AGAINST THE GRAIN

BOOKS BY THE SAME AUTHOR

Revenue System in post-Maurya and Gupta Times (1967)

Ancient India (1977, 1998, 2015)

Economy and Society in Early India: Issues and Paradigms (1993)

Holy Cow: Beef in Indian Dietary Traditions (2001)
reprinted as *The Myth of the Holy Cow* (2002, 2004, 2009)

Early India (2004)

Rethinking Hindu Identity (2009)

EDITED WORKS

Society and Ideology in India: Essays in Honour of Prof. R.S. Sharma (1993)

The Feudal Order (2001)

Mind and Matter: Essays on Mentalities in Medieval India jointly with Eugenia Vanina (2009)

The Many Careers of D.D. Kosambi (2011)

Contesting Symbols and Stereotypes: Essays on Indian History and Culture (2013)

The Complex Heritage of Early India (2014)

The Evolution of a Nation: Precolonial to Postcolonial (2014)

AGAINST THE GRAIN

Notes on Identity, Intolerance and History

D. N. JHA

MANOHAR
2023

First published 2018
Reprinted 2021, 2022, 2023

ISBN 978-93-5098-168-9 (Hb)
ISBN 978-93-88540-12-4 (Pb)

Published by
Ajay Kumar Jain *for*
Manohar Publishers & Distributors
4753/23 Ansari Road, Daryaganj
New Delhi 110 002

Printed at
Replika Press Pvt. Ltd.

To the memory of
my mother, Gauri Devi (d. 1945)
who left me in my childhood and could not
give me her love and affection in full measure;
and my father, Devaswarup Jha (d. 1977),
who compensated for this loss and instilled
in me a preference for reason over faith.

ये नाम केचिदिह नः प्रथयन्त्यवज्ञां
जानन्ति ते किमपि तान्प्रति नैष यत्नः ।
उत्पत्स्यते तु मम कोऽपि समानधर्मा
कालो ह्ययं निरवधिर्विपुला च पृथ्वी ।।

Those who deride or ignore my work –
let them know: my efforts are not for them.
There will come along someone who shares my spirit:
the world is vast, and time endless.

From *Malatimadhavam* by Bhavabhuti

Bol, yeh thodaa waqt bahut hai
Jism-o-zubaan ki maut se pehle
Bol, ke sach zindaa hai ab tak
Bol, jo kuch kehnaa hai keh-le!

The short time left to you
is still enough. Speak up!
Before the body
and its tongue give out.
Speak out!
For truth still survives
Speak out!
Say whatever you have to say!

From 'Bol' by Faiz Ahmed Faiz

Contents

Preface

WHEN INDIA BECAME independent from British rule in 1947, the consequent jubilation was marred by the devastation of the country's partition into India and Pakistan leading to unprecedented miseries – riots, mass casualties, and a colossal wave of migration. But at the same time policy framers and nation builders, led by Jawaharlal Nehru and inspired by his 'tryst with destiny' speech, were able to establish a secular and socialist state. Its most urgent task was the national reconstruction which required not only a relentless activity at the legislative and administrative level but also an intense academic debate on the daunting issues facing it. Caste and untouchability, poverty of the people, the country's economy which the British had left in a shambles, the trauma of partition and the subsequent communal conflagrations were some of the problems that dominated the post Independence discourse in social sciences. In history this meant a reassessment of India's past which necessitated a rigorous scrutiny of sources and their use on scientific and secular lines. Thus in the post-independence period the textual sources have been used with much greater attention to their chronology, content and geography than was the case earlier; artifacts and antiquities which satisfied the antiquarian appetite of archaeologists have now become a major source for the study of material culture, patterns of rural / urban settlements, technology, etc. The interaction between history and other disciplines like sociology and anthropology has enriched historical research methodologically as well as by raising new issues and expanding its scope. Thus history has become a scientific enterprise during the decades after Independence.

But of late, with the Hindutva onslaught, scientific and secular history has received a major setback. Reason is overwhelmed by obscurantism; rational analysis is succumbing to blind faith. A revival by the Hindu Right of colonial view of India's past is quite evident. That India has no history was first asserted by the British but it is now endorsed by the Hindutva votaries who are questioning the very necessity of having a history; if there is any need for it, they tell us, the epics, *Ramayana* and *Mahabharata*, should suffice as true histories! Thus myth masquerades as truth and mystery as history. The image of India as a stagnant society, first projected by the British, has received endorsement from the Hindutva ideologues who take pride in its uninterrupted continuity from the beginning which they often trace to geological time. The stereotype of Hindus as spiritualistic and tolerant people, based on imperialist writings, is giving rise to weird ideas which easily receive popular acceptance. The Hindutva enthusiasts, not surprisingly, consider themselves spiritual preceptors of the world so much so that the Indian prime minister does not hesitate to welcome foreign dignitaries with a copy of the *Gita*, which is more a book of fratricidal war than of a consistent philosophical system. Hinduism has become extremely exclusive and Muslims and Christians, whose religions originated outside India, are being steadily denied a dignified place in this country. The Hindu Right wing organizations are keen on establishing a Hindu state in India which has generated a spurious debate on nationalism. Muslims are lynched on mere suspicion of carrying and eating beef and so are the dalits whose livelihood depends on skinning a dead cow. All this has the direct or indirect backing of the Indian state whose anti-intellectualism needs to be questioned and combated. The present collection of essays is a modest step in this direction. The highbrow academics may dismiss it as polemical and may not find anything new here. But the papers in this short volume are addressed to the people vulnerable to the balderdash peddled by the Hindu Right; the trenchant lines from the poem 'Bol' by the late Faiz Ahmed Faiz at the start of the book captures the rebellious spirit underlying the present anthology.

The papers presented here have been written over the past few years, especially during the ascendancy of the Rashtriya Swayamsevak Sangh and the political, cultural and religious organizations affiliated to it. Some of these papers have been published earlier in newspapers and books; others have appeared in the form of press interviews on contentious issues of contemporary India. Due acknowledgement has been made to them at the appropriate places. There are a few papers which have not been published earlier. The use of diacritical marks for Sanskrit words has been avoided throughout. Keeping the ease of reading in view, notes and references have been given as endnotes.

I thank Dr Jyotsna Arora and Ms Malvika Gulati of the Indian Concil of Historical Research, New Delhi, for their indispensable bibliographical assistance and Professor Anjani Kumar Sinha for advice from time to time. Ramesh Jain and Siddharth Chowdhury deserve special thanks for seeing the volume through the press.

D.N. Jha

New Delhi
3 November 2017

ONE

Prehistory of Hindu Identity*

THE HINDUTVA IDEOLOGUES would like us to believe that the religion called Hinduism has been in existence since eternity, but a rational analysis attributes its emergence to a very recent period. The term 'Hindooism' was first used by Charles Grant in 1787[1] but by the late nineteenth century it became a full-fledged colonial construct when the British rulers undertook the census operations from 1872. They applied the categories of 'Hindus' and 'Muhammadans' to classify and divide the people of the Indian colony on religious lines. This division suited the imperial policy of divide and rule but, more importantly, fueled the constant conflict between the Hindus and Muslims and other religious groups and created the notion of a Hindu identity as distinct from Muslim or Christian.

Another important factor that led to the creation of a Hindu identity was the acceptance and dissemination of the term 'Hinduism' by the Indian religious thinkers and

*This paper draws substantially on my article published in D.N. Jha, ed., *Contesting Symbols and Stereotypes*, Delhi, 2011.

reformists of the nineteenth century which represents the initial phase of its history. Among them Raja Rammohun Roy (1772-1833), who founded the Brahmo Samaj in 1828, was the first to use the term 'Hindooism' in 1816.[2] He advocated Hinduism and was against the expansion of Christianity, even though he was in favour of certain Western reformist ideas like the abolition of sati. The religion based on the Vedas and Upanishads, he argued, was monotheistic and egalitarian, and it was only in course of time that decline set in and retrograde practices like polytheism, caste system and the suppression of women crept into it. The notion of the Vedic period as a 'golden age' was thus 'embodied in the doctrine of the Brahmo Samaj'[3] which anticipated the ideas of subsequent religious reformers like Dayananda Saraswati (1824-83).

Dayananda Saraswati founded the reformist organization Arya Samaj in 1875, and like Roy, he too harked back to the Vedic golden age in Aryavarta where the first man was born and where Sanskrit, the mother of all tongues, was spoken;[4] he also 'maintained that the "Aryas" of the Vedas were the autochthonous people of Bharat'.[5] Unlike Roy, however, he treated the Vedas as a divine revelation and accorded them the status of a fixed and clearly demarcated canon – a status which the Bible and Koran enjoyed in Christianity and Islam respectively. This gave a 'specifity and distinction' to the Arya Samajist ideology in relation to Hinduism which, according to it, was a degraded form of Vedic religion – a reason why the followers of Dayananda preferred to register themselves as 'Aryas' and not Hindus in the 1891 Punjab census.[6]

Apparently thus Dayananda would not initially appear to be a proponent of Hindu nationalism but, judging from his activities, he was certainly a forerunner of the later Hindu chauvinism and xenophobia. For example, he fully supported the militant Hinduism's concern for cow-protection, and founded the Gorakshini Sabha in 1882. His commitment to the movement for cow-protection was so strong that despite his sharp ideological differences with the adherents of the anti-reformist and orthodox brahminical religious practices called the Sanatanists, the Arya Samajists felt no uneasiness of conscience in collaborating with them over the issue. The idea of protecting the cow thus gained popularity among a wide cross-section of the people and galvanized and unified them as Hindus.[7] It strengthened their separate identity as against that of the Muslims who were stereotyped as kine killers and beef eaters.

Dayananda regarded as enemies those who or whose ancestors had converted to Islam and Christianity[8] and led the movement for their purification/reconversion (*shuddhi*). His missionary activity was initially opposed by the orthodox Sanatanists who projected Hinduism as a non-proselytising religion,[9] but it soon received their endorsement, notably from persons like Madan Mohan Malaviya, in the early twentieth century. This further tended to reinforce the idea of Hindu identity.

Some of the ideas of Dayananda were repeated by Vivekananda (1863-1902), who, like him, glorified the Vedas and Upanishads, and referred nostalgically to the earliest period of Indian past as one of 'Vedic harmony' –

a period when the people were 'ruled according to the principles of the Vedas and India enjoyed 2000 years of uninterrupted peace, tranquility and prosperity';[10] in contrast, he spoke, with a *cri de coeur*, of the period of the Muslim rule as one of the oppression of the Hindus.[11] He did not share the concern of Dayananda for cow-protection and, even advised 'young men in India to eat beef in order to develop muscles',[12] but like him, he was interested in converting members of other faiths to his own Advaita Vedanta and which he used assidously to unify the Hindus. He founded the Rama Krishna Mission in 1897 for its promotion and propagation through *maths* and *ashrams* in different parts of India as well as through international proselytizing activity.[13]

Despite their different views on issues relating to the social and religious reform, Dayananda and Vivekananda shared a revivalist perception of India's past and an exclusivist notion of Hinduism, which were echoed by their contemporaries in different parts of the country. In Bengal, for example, Rajnarain Basu (1826-99), a close associate of Debendranath Tagore, stood for the glory of Sanatana Dharma and spoke aggressively of the superiority of Hindu religion and culture in contrast to Christainity and Islam. He asserted that 'his Hindu Mahasamiti could not have a place for Muslims'.[14] Chandranath Basu (1844-1910), who was intimate to Bankim Chandra Chattopadhyaya and was a champion of reform through revivalism, published his *Hindutva: An Authentic History of Hindus* in Bengali in 1892 in which he portrayed Hinduism 'in terms of its glorious archaic past' and as superior to Christianity; he also presented his spirited defense of traditional brahminical ritualism, child marriage, caste system, patriarchal values, etc. Essentially anti-Islamist at the core, the Hindutva[15] idea popularized by him was conspicuously present in Bankim Chandra's (1838-94) influential novel *Anandamath* (1882), which refers to Muslims as 'dirty bastards'.[16]

The demonization of Muslims was a prominent theme also in the works of writers outside Bengal. Bharatendu Harishchandra (1850-85), born in Banaras and considered to be the father of modern Hindi literature, depicted Muslim characters in his works as cruel, cowardly, treacherous, bigots and uniformly depraved; his contemporaries described Muslim rule 'as a chronicle of rape and abduction of Hindu women, the slaughter of sacred cows, and the defilement of temples'.[17] A similar portrayal of Muslims is found in the works of the Marathi writers who described them as 'bullies and fanatics' and the period of their rule as one of 'the overall degradation of the Hindus' and of the spread of the 'pernicious influence of Islam on their social customs'.[18] The most influential among them was the nationalist and social reformer Bal Gangadhar Tilak (1856-1920) who strengthened the notion of a Hindu identity through 'a conscious choice of historical figures and symbols'.[19] His reinvention of a largely domestic festival of Ganesh by giving it a group character was intended to mobilize the Hindus just as his promotion of festivals of Shivaji revived his memories and projected him as a pre-eminent symbol of Hindu militancy against Muslims. In 1893 he founded the Anti-Cow Killing Society and gave a direct challenge to Muslims. While Tilak thus sought to build an aggressive Maratha/Hindu identity leading often to Hindu-Muslim tension, he emphatically asserted that the essence of Hinduism lay in its metaphysics and tolerance of other faiths,[20] though judging by his anti-Muslim sentiments and activities, these were mere empty words.

Tilak's writings on the history of ancient Indian culture[21] dwelt on the Hindu-Aryan primordialism and supported his notion of a Hindu nation. He pushed the date of the Vedic period from 1500 BC first to 4000 BC and then to 8000 BC, glorified the Vedic Aryan race and religion and wove 'a thread of cultural and religious continuity between the Aryans of the furthest antiquity and present-day Hindus'.[22] Despite his view that the original home of the Aryans was in the Arctic, he underlined the importance of the Vedic Aryan heritage. 'During Vedic times', Tilak asserted, 'India was a self-contained country ... united as a great nation....' He contended that the 'common factor' in Indian society was 'the feeling of Hindutva' and that all 'hindus were one because of their adherence to *Hindudharma*'.[23] Based on his reading of the *Bhagvadgita,* on which he wrote an elaborate commentary, he espoused the use of violence as a higher duty.[24] Tilak's ideas, especially his anti-Muslim sentiments, assertion of Aryan/Hindu primordiality, and his apologia for the use of violence had many takers during the extremist phase of India's freedom struggle. The most important of them was Shri Aurobindo, who declared that the Hindu religion was the eternal religion (*sanatana dharma*) preserved by the Aryan race through centuries. He equated it with nationalism. Like Tilak, he was inspired by the *Gita* and justified the use of violence in the nationalist resistance to the British rule.[25] It was, however, Tilak who was really the forerunner of militant Hinduism of the subsequent years expounded by V.D. Savarkar (1883-1966), K.B. Hedgewar (1889-1940), M.S. Golwalkar (1906-73) and others in the wake of an unprecedented communalization of Indian politics from the 1920s onwards.

V.D. Savarkar, seven-time president of the the Right-wing political party, Hindu Mahasabha, and founder of the modern day Hindutva movement, sought to provide a comprehensive definition of Hindu identity in his *Hindutva: Who is a Hindu?* published in 1923. Although he borrowed and elaborated several ideas of Tilak with whom he came in contact early in life, the latter's commitment to anti-cow slaughter movement was not much of an attraction for Savarkar but it was the Hindutva idea of Tilak which became the central theme of his work. He postulated that it was Hindutva (= Hinduness), rather than Hinduism, that constituted Hindu identity. But Hindutva itself, he tells us, 'defies all attempts at analysis – [it] is not a word but a history. Not only the spiritual or religious history of our people, but a history in full.'[26] Like Tilak, he accepted the idea that the Aryans originated outside India, migrated into the modern Punjab and called themselves Hindu (or Sindhu) for the first time and spread out to different parts of the subcontinent with their civilization, giving birth to a common race of the Hindus through miscegenation of Aryans and non-Aryans, and creating new 'colonies' on the way till the day Rama made his triumphant entry into Ceylon, the day which was 'the real birth-day of our Hindu people'.[27] On the one hand Savarkar dated the Hindu identity to a period 'that even mythology fails to penetrate'[28] and thus primordialized it; and, on the other, he declared that it was during the medieval period that Hindus were welded into a nation as a result of their 'struggle' against the 'Muslim invaders' and 'tyrants'.

Savarkar's perception of history was deeply flawed but he insisted that Hindus are a nation and India must be a land reserved for them. A Hindu, according to Savarkar, was one (i) who acquired citizenship by paternal descent, i.e. who was born in India, (ii) who was born of Hindu parents and thus possessed Vedic Aryan blood and; (iii) who shared a common *sanskriti* (culture) '... suggestive ... of that language, Sanskrit, which has been the chosen means of expression and preservation of that culture, of all that was best and worth-preserving in the history of our race'.[29] In the ultimate analysis, a Hindu, according to him, was one who regarded India as his fatherland (*pitribhumi*) and holy land (*punyabhumi*),[30] one whose religion must have grown 'out of the soil of India'. This definition of a Hindu was exclusive and did not include Muslims and Christians whose holy lands were in Arabia and Palestine respectively. Savarkar's Hindu supremacism was best summed up in his call to 'Hinduise all politics and Militarise all Hindudom' – a call that was to become a rallying cry of Hindu identity and nationalism.

Two years after Savarkar expounded his concept of Hindutva, Keshav Baliram Hedgewar, a Maharashtrian brahmin of Tilakite association, proclaimed that long before the recorded history, the Hindus were a mighty and prosperous nation and they ruled 'over vast regions of the earth and our flag flew over many lands...'.[31] But his real importance in promoting militant Hindu identity lay not in his ideas articulated through his occasional writings and speeches but in the fact that in 1925 he founded the Rashtriya Swayamsevak Sangh (National Volunteer Corps), popularly known as the RSS, whose network has grown steadily over the years and has now a large number of bodies including political parties affiliated to it.[32] This organization, with its proto-martial character, has remained the vanguard of the Hindutva movement and has had its hand, directly or through its affiliates, in many communal conflagrations.[33]

While Savarkar provided an ideological *raison d'être* of the RSS, Hedgewar gave it a para-military and fascist character. It was, however, for M.S. Golwalkar, who succeeded him in 1940 as chief of the RSS, to give it 'the ideological charter it had previously lacked'.[34] In 1939, a year before he took over from Hedgewar as the second chief of the RSS, he published his *We or Our Nationhood Defined*;[35] a collection of his essays and speeches came out in 1966 as *Bunch of Thoughts*.

While Savarkar had already claimed that the Hindu race originated four thousand years ago, now Golwalkar, much like Tilak, pushed its antiquity to 80-100 centuries. Inspired by Hitler's ethnic nationalism he rejected the view that the Hindu-Aryans have been exogenous to India and asserted that 'we Hindus came into this land from nowhere, but are indigenous children of the soil always, from time immemorial and are natural masters of the country…'.[36] It was from this indigenist Hindu-Aryan position that he asserted that

> the foreign races in Hindusthan [*sic*] must either adopt the Hindu culture and language, must learn to respect and hold in reverence Hindu religion, must entertain no ideas but those of glorification of the Hindu race and culture … or may stay in the country, wholly subordinated to the Hindu nation, claiming nothing, deserving no privileges, far less any preferential treatment – not even citizen's rights.[37]

Deeply committed to the supremacy of the Hindu religion and culture, Golwalkar enunciated his notion of 'cultural nationalism' which was distinct from Savarkar's 'territorial nationalism' and which, in his scheme of things, made it obligatory for Muslims and other religious minorities to respect and revere the Hindu religion. Unlike Savarkar, he attached great importance to the protection of cow and considered this animal as 'mother' and the emblem of Hindu devotion and protested against its slaughter.[38] According to him, the Muslims began the practice of cow killing in India and the Britishers continued it and since the practice began with foreign domination 'it is a stigma on us'.[39] Despite some differences in their ideas and attitudes, both Savarkar and Golwalkar emphasized, in varying degrees, the primordialization and indigenization of Hindu identity. They also demonized religious minorities, especially the Muslims – a tendency whose pugnacious manifestations culminated in the demolition of the sixteenth century Muslim mosque at Ayodhya in 1992 triggering countrywide communal riots and the genocide of Muslims in Gujarat in 2002. Even so the RSS and its affiliates loudly proclaim that Hinduism is a 'universalistic and tolerant religious philosophy',[40] though the chicanery, deception and trickery underlying such a claim are all too clear from the present RSS chief Mohan Bhagwat's repeated passionate appeal to turn India into a Hindu nation.

The divisive concept of Hindu identity propagated by the social and religious reformers, nationalist leaders and cultural nationalists has received much institutional support from modern university system and has found a prominent place in academic histories since the early twentieth century – a fact which calls for a separate detailed study but an example or two should be enough to illustrate the point. Thus the Calcutta University, the first modern university in India, established separate departments of ancient Indian history and culture and Islamic history; the first gave a boost to the supposed glories of ancient India and the second to the denigration of Muslims. In order to highlight Hindu resistance to them the Calcutta University also introduced separate courses on the history of Rajputs, Marathas and Sikhs who all fought against the Mughals. Many universities established subsequently followed suit and set up separate departments for the teaching and research in ancient Indian history and culture. This discouraged the study of an integrated history of the country, and encouraged the growth of a retrograde and revivalist historiography with primordialization and glorification of the Aryan/Hindu identity as its main agenda. Thus almost at the same time as Savarkar was busy defining the contours of Hindu identity, Abinash Chandra Das, a lecturer in ancient Indian history and culture in Calcutta University, argued that the Aryans were the original inhabitants of Sapta-Sindhu (modern Punjab) which, according to him, was 'the oldest life-producing region in the whole of the Indian subcontinent', and assigned the Rigvedic hymns to 25,000 years ago or the Pleistocene.[41]

A majority of historians writing during the period of nationalist resistance to the British rule as well as after India's Independence have oddly clung not only to the ideas of autochthony and fantastic antiquity of the Aryans but also to their supposed civilizing role in the ancient world. According to them the ancient Indians transmitted a 'high culture to a melange of unlettered primitives' and established colonies in many Asian countries like Burma, Java, Cambodia, Bali and Vietnam. A major source of inspiration to these historians has been the notion of a Greater India in ancient times, promoted by the Greater India Society founded in Calcutta in 1926 with the objective of organizing the study of the history and culture of Asian countries in which ancient Indians supposedly established colonies. A person no less than Rabindranath Tagore was its *purodha* (spiritual head), but many scholars extended active support to it.[42]

Among the scholars associated with the Greater India Society, the historian R.C. Majumdar was the most influential, industrious and prolific; not surprisingly cultural nationalists and Hindu supremacists have often derived legitimacy from his revivalist and anti-Islamist writings. A persistent apologist of the greatness of ancient 'Hindus' and a firm believer in the Hinduization of the South-East Asian countries, he ignored their indigenous cultures and thus lent an ideological support to Hedgewar's vacuous claim that the Hindu 'flag flew over many lands'. As general editor of the multi-volume Bharatiya Vidya Bhavan publication, *History and Culture of the Indian People*, Majumdar devoted more volumes to what he considered to be the periods of Hindu domination and less volumes to those that were in his view phases of Muslim ascendancy.[43] He credited the Hindus for their 'spirit of religious toleration' and denigrated the Muslims for their intolerant and oppressive rule and for destroying Hindu temples.

A similar anti-Muslim attitude is seen in the works of Jadunath Sarkar who wrote extensively on medieval Indian history. Like Majumdar, he perceived the medieval period as one of perpetual confrontation between the Hindus and Muslims and, asserted that the ideal of the Mughal state was 'the conversion of the entire population to Islam'. Listing all the individual acts of omission and commission during the 'Muslim rule', he presented a profoundly negative picture of Muslim rulers[44] and spoke in glowing terms of the resistance to Muslims by Shivaji who emerged as a symbol of Maratha/Hindu chauvinism. Shivaji of course has now become a significant factor in even contemporary Indian politics – so much so that any critical reference to him may prove perilous! Majumdar, Sarkar and other scholars of their ilk have projected the Muslims as oppressors, and inherently intolerant of Hindus who, by contrast, are perceived as weak and tolerant. The latter feared the former and, according to an influential and respected historian, the Hindu women adopted the custom of veiling after AD 1200 so as to protect themselves 'from the covetous eyes of the [Muslim] soldiery' – a view patently erroneous but deeply embedded in popular consciousness. [45] Muslims, we are also told, are vastly different from Hindus not only in religious beliefs and practices but also dietary culture and social customs. The former have been stereotyped as beef eaters as against Hindus who are all thought of as vegetarians;[46] cow has thus become the most political animal in today's India.

The demonization of Muslims by some modern historians has thus fed into the dialectic of the aggressive Hindu identity. But its cheerleaders remain the militant Hindutva organizations affiliated to the RSS which have created many myths and misconceptions about it, including the fiction of an eternal Hinduism. According to the website of the Vedic Foundation based in the US, the Indian/Hindu civilization has existed in the Ganga valley uninterruptedly since 1972 million years![47]

The RSS and its mushrooming affiliates, have been receiving considerable support from the misuse of electronic media which over the years have given a boost to spurious religiosity through their numerous channels beaming religious soap operas – a trend which began in the late 1980s when the state owned Indian television made a major departure from its well established secular policy and telecast two Hindu religious epics, *Ramayana* and *Mahabharata.* The televising of these epics between 1987 and 1989 coincided with the crescendo of the Hindutva cry for the 'liberation' of several Hindu pilgrimage centres, especially Ayodhya, where the Sangh Parivar and its extended family later demolished the sixteenth century mosque.

The Hindu fanatics keep parroting that Ayodhya is the birth place of Rama. Even their senior most leader L.K. Advani, allegedly involved in the demolition of the mosque on 6 December 1992, unabashedly asserted:

> Sri Rama is the unique symbol, the unequalled symbol of our oneness, or our integration, as well as of our aspiration to live the higher values. As Maryada Purushottam Sri Rama has represented for thousands of years the ideal of conduct, just as Rama Rajya has represented the ideal of governance.[48]

This is no different from a loud proclamation of the RSS chief, according to whom a temple to Rama would establish the country's 'self-identity'.[49] Rama is thus a hinduized and nationalized hero; he is the most political god of India today. Rama, like the cow, has become a means to consolidate and mobilize the Hindus for the capture of political power and retaining it as Narendra Modi has been doing for the last few years.

The Hindutva efforts to homogenize Hindu religious beliefs and practices by projecting Rama as the god above other gods and the *Ramayana* as the scripture over other religious texts have gone alongside a strong censorship of some important and interesting aspects of Indian culture and history. In 1993, not long after the Sangh Parivar and its goons demolished the mosque at Ayodhya, they attacked the Sahmat exhibition consisting of panels on the different versions of the Rama legend, especially the one on the Buddhist text, *Dasharatha Jataka*, which depicts Rama and Sita as brother and sister. The vandalization of the panel followed by its banning by the Delhi government at the instance of L.K. Advani and other BJP leaders[50] amounted to a denial of the plurality of the *Ramayana* tradition. It was also a total rejection of the Buddhist origin myths according to which 'the founding family of ancient Indian "republics" resulted from an incestuous union between brother and sister'.[51] A few years later, in 1998, the Hindutva hoodlums demonstrated against Deepa Mehta's film, *Fire*, whose story revolved round the same-sex love, though it is not unknown in ancient Indian literature. The most important example of censorship in contemporary India by Hindu extremists is that of the paintings by Maqbool Fida Husain, who was unquestionably the greatest painter of modern India. In 1996 they questioned the legitimacy of nudity in Hindu religious art and raised a huge hue and cry over the depiction of Hindu goddesses in nude by Husain,[52] 'a Muslim artist'. Combining the 'coercive use of law' with threats of various kinds, the Hindutva elements forced Husain to leave the country and die in exile. He became a victim as much of communal politics as of the cultural terrorism unleashed by the Hindu fanatics.[53]

The Hindu extremists have also tried to appropriate and even invent cultural symbols of questionable Hindu association. For instance, when, in 2005, the European

Union initiated the move to ban the Swastika, a reminder of the Holocaust, the Indian diaspora strongly protested and claimed the symbol as the 'most ancient and Hindu', despite its provenance in different parts of the ancient world. At home, they have been distributing tridents (*trishulas*), Shiva's weapon, in different states of India, and have called it *trishula-diksha* (initiation through tridents). The trident is not specifically Indian; possibly an import from the north-west, its association with Shiva is very late. The *trishula-diksha* is likewise unknown to Indian tradition, and is an invention of the Sangh Parivar. Though projected as a venture of 'glorious cultural resurgence' to reinvigorate the 'Hindu' ethos, it is, in reality, an effort to symbolically weaponize the Hindus against religious minorities.

The Hindutva ideologues and their foot soldiers have been trying to redefine the boundaries of Hinduism, and examples of this can be multiplied to almost any length. They censure anything that does not fit into their scheme. They burn books that do not endorse their view, vandalize objects of art which they consider blasphemous, and demonstrate against films which present a counter point to their propaganda. They distort Indian history and religion and nurture a culture of intolerance. They lynch any one on mere suspicion of eating beef or transporting cows to abattoirs. These traits have become all the more pronounced with the political ascendancy of the Bharatiya Janata Party (BJP) and its mentor the RSS during the last few years. Hindu identity has now become a Frankenstein's monster for all that is truly Indian.

NOTES

1. Will Sweetman, *Mapping Hinduism: Hinduism and the Study of Indian Religions 1600-1776*, Halle, 2003, p. 56, n. 12. In 1787 too, William Jones used the term 'Hindu' in the religious sense (S.N. Mukherjee, *Sir William Jones and British Attitudes to India,* Cambridge, 1968, p. 119).
2. Dermot Killingley, *Rammohun Roy in Hindu and Christian Tradition: The Teape Lectures 1990*, Newcastle upon Tyne, 1993, p. 60.
3. Christopher Jaffrelot, *Hindu Nationalism: A Reader,* Delhi, 2007, pp. 7-8.
4. J.T.F. Jordens, *Dayanand Saraswati: His Life and Ideas*, Delhi, 1978, p. 110.
5. Jaffrelot, *Hindu Nationalism*, p. 9.
6. K. Jones, 'Religious Identity and the Indian Census', in N.G. Barrier, ed., *The Census in British India*, Delhi, 1981, p. 87.
7. John Zavos, *The Emergence of Hindu Nationalism*, Delhi, 2000, pp. 87-8.
8. J.E. Llewellyn, *The Arya Samaj as a Fundamentalist Movement*, Delhi, 1993, pp. 99-103; Zavos, op. cit., pp. 87-92.
9. Since caste system (*varnashramadharma*) has always occupied a central position in the orthodox sanatanist Hindu religion, and since the Arya Samajist ideology preached the necessity to recognize merit-based caste and not the traditional hereditary caste system, questions were raised about how a convert could be looked upon as a Hindu unless he or she was assigned a place in the caste hierarchy. This added a controversial dimension to *shuddhi* (reconversion) but in the early twentieth century leaders like Madan Mohan Malaviya lent support to this movement (Jaffrelot, *Hindu Nationalism,* pp. 68-9).
10. Amalendu Misra, *Identity and Religion: Foundations of Anti-Islamism in India*, Delhi, 2004, p. 37.
11. Vivekananda's hostility towards Muslims is evident from this statement: 'from Pacific to the Atlantic for five hundred years blood ran all over the world ... that is Mohammadanism' (Shakespeare club of Pasadena, California, USA, on 3 February 1900).

12. Jyotirmaya Sharma, *Cosmic Love and Human Apathy: Swami Vivekananda's Restatement of Religion*, Delhi, 2013, p. 272.
13. Torkel Brekke, *Makers of Modern Indian Religion in the Nineteenth Century*, New York, 2002, p. 47.
14. Chetan Bhatt, *Hindu Nationalism, Ideologies and Modern Myths*, Berg, 2001, p. 24.
15. The word 'Hindutva' was first mentioned by Panchanana Tarkaratana in 1840 in the context of the debate generated by John Muir.
16. Tanika Sarkar, 'Imaginning Hindu Rashtra: The Hindu and the Muslim in Bankim Chandra's Writings', in David Ludden, ed., *Making India Hindu*, Delhi, 1996, p. 175. This portrayal of Muslims, however, was contested by intellectuals like Bhudev Mukhopadhyaya (1827-94) and others (Mushirul Hasan, 'The Myth of Unity: Colonial and National Narratives', in David Ludden, op. cit., p. 201.)
17. Hasan, op. cit., p. 200
18. Ibid., p. 200.
19. Ibid.
20. Shanta Sathe, *Lokmanya Tilaka: His Social and Political Thoughts*, Delhi, 1994, p.166.
21. Bal Gangadhar Tilak authored several books, the most well-known of them being the *Orion or Researches into the Antiquity of the Vedas* (1893), *Arctic Home in the Vedas* (1903) and the *Gitarahasya* (1915).
22. Vasant Kaiwar, 'The Aryan Model of History and the Oriental Renaissance: The Politics of Identity in an Age of Revolutions, Colonialism and Nationalism', in Vasant Kaiwar and Sucheta Mazumdar, eds., *Antinomies of Modernity: Essays on Race, Orient, Nation*, Delhi, 2003, p. 45.
23. Bhatt, op. cit, p. 36; Kaiwar, op. cit, p. 45.
24. Robert N. Minor, *Modern Indian Interpreters of the Bhagvadgita,* Delhi, 1991, pp. 44-60.
25. Kaiwar, op. cit., p. 42; Minor, op. cit., pp. 61-87.
26. V.D. Savarkar, *Hindutva: Who is a Hindu?,* Delhi, 2005 [1923], p. 3.
27. Savarkar, ibid., pp. 11-12; Bhatt, op. cit., p. 87.
28. Savarkar, ibid., p. 10.

29. Ibid., p. 92.
30. Ibid., p. 115
31. Pralay Kanungo, *RSS's Tryst with Politics: From Hedgewar to Sudarshan*, Delhi, 2002, p. 42.
32. Jaffrelot, *The Nationalist Movement and Indian Politics 1925 to the 1990s*, Delhi, 1996; idem., *Sangh Parivar*. Also see Dhirendra K. Jha, *The Shadow Armies,* Delhi, 2017.
33. The martial brand of Hinduism represented by the RSS is buttressed by its hierachical and dictatorial organizational structure, and the daily morning/evening meeting of its basic unit called *shakhas* (branch) where the young recruits are imparted physical and mental training more or less on the model of the traditional *akhara*, a place where 'the young men of a locality gather daily for body building, exercise and sports – mainly wrestling and weight-lifting' (Jaffrelot, *Sangh Parivar*, pp. 2-5, 56-102).
34. Ibid., p. 97.
35. Some years ago the RSS and the Hindu Right-wing parties tried to dissociate themselves from Golwalkar's book. But this has been based on falsehoods which generally go with their functioning. (Shamsul Islam, *Golwalkar's We or Our Nationhood Defined: A Critique with the Text of the Book*, Delhi, 2006, pp. 44-52).
36. M.S. Golwalkar, *We or Our Nationhood Defined*, Nagpur, 1939, p. 6.
37. Ibid.
38. Golwalkar, *Bunch of Thoughts*, Bangalore, 1966, pp. 59, 232, 363.
39. Ibid., p. 496.
40. Kanungo, op. cit., p. 126.
41. A.C. Das, *Rgvedic India,* Calcutta, 1971 [1920], pp. 22-3.
42. Susan Bayly, 'Imagining "Greater India": French and Indian Visions of Colonialism in the Indic Mode', *Modern Asian Studies*, vol. 38, no. 3 (2004), pp. 703-44. Among scholars directly involved in the establishment and activities of the Geater India Society were P.C. Bagchi, Suniti Kumar Chatterji, Phanindra Nath Bose, Kalidas Nag, U.N. Ghoshal, Nalinaksha Datta and R.C. Majumdar. The list of other well known historians who unequivocally supported the notion of a Greater India in ancient times would

be long but notable among them are K.P. Jayaswal, H.C. Raichaudhari, K.A. Nilakanta Sastri, to name only a few.

43. R.S. Sharma, 'Communalism and India's Past', *Social Scientist,* vol. 18, nos. 1-2 (1990), p. 6.
44. S.K. Srivastava, *Sir Jadunath Sarkar: The Historian at Work*, Delhi, 1989, p. 86. For a recent reassessment of Sarkar's historiography see Dipesh Chakrabarty, *The Calling of History: Sir Jadunath Sarkar and his Empire of Truth*, Chicago, 2015.
45. Many pre-Islamic Sanskrit texts refer to the veiling of women. The word *avagunthana* (veil), for instance, occurs in the *Ramayana* of Valmiki, *Mudrarakshasa* of Vishakhadatta, *Mrichhakañika* of Shudraka, *Abhijnanashakuntalam* and *Kumarasambhava* of Kalidasa, and *Venisamhara* of Bhattanarayana, etc. Pratibha Patil, the presidential candidate, was obviously ill advised to state publicly on 18 June 2007, that 'the purdah system was introduced to protect them [women] from the Muslim invaders', *The Indian Express*, 19 June 2007.
46. A specialist in medieval Indian history tells us that the 'Hindus in general were vegetarians ... and abhorred beef' and the Muhammadans, on the other hand, 'were almost cent per cent non-vegetarians, and were not prepared to give up cow slaughter and beef-eating' (A.L. Srivastava, *The Sultanate of Delhi 711-1526*, Agra, 1984).
47. See the website of the Vedic Foundation (USA). http://www.thevedicfoundation.org/the_true_history_and_the_religion_of_india/index.html
48. BJP White Paper, 1993.
49. *The Hindu*, 8 February 2013.
50. Rajeev Dhavan, 'Ban, Burn and Destroy', *Outlook*, 23 January 2004.
51. Romila Thapar, *A History of India,* vol. 1, Penguin, 1992 [1966], p. 51; idem, *Early India: From Origins to AD 1300*, Berkeley, 2002, p. 148.
52. The Husain controversy was triggered by Om Nagpal's article 'Ye Chitrakar Hai Ya Kasai', published in *Vichar Mimansa*, September 1996. For a discussion of its various aspects see Monica Juneja, 'Reclaiming the Public Sphere: Husain's Portrayals of

Saraswati and Draupadi', *Economic and Political Weekly*, vol. 32, no. 4, 25-31 January 1997, pp. 155-7. Tapati Guha-Thakurta, *Monuments, Objects, Histories: Institutions of Art in Colonial and Postcolonial India,* New Delhi, 2004, pp. 245-6. Rajeev Dhavan, *Harassing Husain: Uses and Abuses of the Law of Hate Speech,* Delhi, 2007.

53. In 2001 when my *Holy Cow: Beef in Indian Dietary Traditions* was published, I was attacked by the Hindutva goons in the Delhi University campus and they succeeded in obtaining a stay on its publication and distribution. But the ban order was defied by getting it published from London as *The Myth of the Holy Cow* (London, 2002).

TWO

Cow Conundrum*

I AM EXTREMELY grateful to the Paschimbanga Itihasa Samsad for giving me the opportunity to deliver this year's lecture in the memory of my respected and beloved teacher Susobhan Chandra Sarkar and to go half a century back in time when I joined the Presidency College, Kolkata, as an undergraduate student. Though a shy, reticent and withdrawn person himself, Susobhan Sarkar was the bellwether of radical and progressive intellectual movement and influenced generations of historians and social scientists through his lectures. I consider it a privilege to have been his pupil and to remember him in the Baker Laboratory where he addressed us for the last time on the occasion of his farewell from the College in 1957.

Professor Susobhan Sarkar taught us nearly the whole gamut of Western history and one of the themes to which he devoted much attention was the religious changes and

*This is an abridged version of my *The Myth of the Holy Cow*, London, 2002. It was delivered as Susobhan Sarkar Memorial Lecture at the Presidency College, Calcutta on 19 August 2008.

conflicts in medieval and early modern Europe. His demystification of religions and religious identities of different groups and his exposition of their inherent intolerance, more than anything else, remain relevant even today. Taking my cue from his lectures on religious conflicts in the Christian world, I propose to draw your attention to the creation of deceptive religious identity on the basis of whether we eat beef or not. As we know, it is often propagated by communal forces that abstention from the killing of cow and eating its flesh is the identity of the Hindus whereas the eating of cow meat is exclusively a mark of Muslim identity. Those who assign a divine status to the bovine sharpen the communal divide in our country, damage its social fabric and strengthen the forces of religious intolerance and bigotry.

I

The communalists who have been raising a hullabaloo over the cow in the political arena do not realize that beef eating remained a fairly common practice for a long time in India and that plentiful evidence for this is available in our own ancient texts and scriptures. The response of historical scholarship to the communal perception of Indian food culture, therefore, has been sober and scholars have drawn attention to the evidence of beef eating which, in fact, begins to be available from the oldest Indian religious text *Rigveda*, supposedly of divine origin. H.H. Wilson, the first occupant of the Chair of Sanskrit at Oxford in 1832, asserted that 'the sacrifice of the horse or of the cow, the gomedha or ashvamedha, appears to have been common in the earliest periods of the Hindu ritual'. Among the Indian scholars who, in the late nineteenth century, put forth most convincingly the view that the practice of killing of cattle at sacrifices and eating their flesh prevailed among the Indo-Aryans was Rajendra Lal Mitra,[1] a product of the Bengal renaissance and described by Rabindranath Tagore as 'the most beloved child of the muse'. Later in the 1940s Mahamahopadhyaya P. V. Kane, a conservative Marathi brahmin and the only Sanskritist to be honoured with the title of Bharatratna, in his multi-volume monumental work *History of Dharmashastra* referred to some Vedic and early Dharmashastric passages which speak of cow killing and beef eating. In 1963, H.D. Sankalia, the father of post-Independence Indian archaeology who possessed a profound knowledge of Sanskrit, drew attention to literary as well as archaeological evidence of eating cattle flesh in ancient India.[2] Similarly, Laxman Shastri Joshi, a Sanskritist of unquestionable scholarship, referred to the Dharmashastra works, which unequivocally support the prevalence of the practice of beef eating in early India.[3] Besides these scholars several other Indian Indologists, not to mention a number of Western scholars, have repeatedly drawn our attention to the textual evidence of eating beef and other types of animal flesh in early India. Curious though it may seem, the Sangh Parivar, has never turned its guns towards them but against historians who have mostly relied on the researches of the above-mentioned distinguished scholars.

II

The early Aryans came to India as a semi-nomadic people with a dominantly pastoral economy with agriculture playing a minimal role in their material life. The *Rigveda,* their earliest text, refers only twenty-one times to agricultural activities. As against this, cattle rearing was a much more important aspect of the early Vedic economy. Cattle were the chief form of wealth and the cow was the most important among them; it was often the cause of inter-tribal wars which were known as *gavishti* (lit. search for cows). The importance of pastoralism in the early Vedic period may be inferred from the fact that according to one view the term for cow (*go*) in its different declensions occurs 176 times in the *Rigveda*;[4] according to another view the cow related terms occur as many as 700 times in the text.[5] The pastoralism, which the Vedic people inherited from their Indo-European past, showed up prominently in different aspects of their life including their religious beliefs and practices.

Like pastoralism, they brought from outside the practice of animal or cattle sacrifice, widely prevalent among the early Aryans. It has been suggested on the basis of linguistic and archaeological evidence that the practice of cattle sacrifice of the Vedic period can be traced to the chronologically earlier steppe cultures of Eastern Europe.[6] Nearer home in ancient Iran through which the eastern branch of Indo-Europeans migrated to India, the *Zend Avesta* bears ample testimony of animal sacrifice and the Vedic term *yajna* (= sacrifice) occurs as *yasna* in the *Avesta* which speaks of the sacrifice of 100 oxen and 1,000 small cattle, in addition to that of 100 horses, 10,000 sheep or goats and 1,000 camels.[7]

Like the *Avesta*, the Vedic texts provide copious evidence of the sacrifice of cattle, horses, sheep, goats and pigs, etc. The *Rigveda* frequently refers to the cooking of the flesh of the ox for offering to gods, especially Indra, the greatest among them, who has some 250 out of more than a thousand hymns dedicated to himself. At one place he is stated to have said: 'they cook for me 15 plus twenty oxen'.[8] At other places he is said to have eaten the flesh of bulls,[9] of one[10] or of a hundred buffaloes[11] or 300 buffaloes roasted by Agni[12] or a thousand buffaloes.[13] Second in importance to Indra is Agni who has some 200 hymns to himself in the *Rigveda*.[14] Unlike the licentious Indra, Agni drank *soma* moderately, his main food being *ghee*. He is described as 'one whose food is the ox and the barren cow',[15] but horses (*ashva*), bulls (*rishabha*), oxen (*ukshana*),[16] barren (?) cows (*vasa*)[17] and rams (*mesha*) were also sacrificed for him.[18] In a passage dealing with the disposal of the dead, clear reference is made 'to the burning of a goat which is the share of Agni, and to the use of the flesh of the cow to protect the body against the flame'.[19] Third in order of importance was the god Soma whose name is derived from a plant which was the source of a heady drink.[20] It has been suggested that 'the fundamental and typical Vedic sacrifices are those of Soma'[21] in which the killing of animals including cattle played a crucial role.[22] There was not much variation in the menu of the Rigvedic gods. Milk, butter, barley, oxen, goats and sheep were their usual food, though some of them had apparently their preferences. Indra, for example, had a special liking for bulls and Pushan, the guardian of the roads, being devoid of teeth, ate mush as a Hobson's choice.[23]

III

The later Vedic texts provide detailed descriptions of sacrifices and frequently refer to ritual cattle slaughter. The *Gopatha Brahmana* alone mentions twenty-one *yajnas*, though all of them may not have required animal killing.[24] A bull (*vrishabha*) was sacrificed to Indra, a dappled cow to the Maruts and a copper coloured cow to the Ashvins. A cow was also sacrificed to Mitra and Varuna.[25] In most of the public sacrifices (e.g. *ashvamedha*, *rajasuya* and the *vajapeya*) flesh of various types of animals, especially that of the cow/ox/bull was required. The *agnyadheya,* which was a preparatory rite preceding all public sacrifices, required a cow to be killed.[26] In the *ashvamedha* (horse sacrifice), the most important of the Vedic public sacrifices, first referred to in the *Rigveda*[27] and later discussed in the Brahmanas, more than 600 animals (including the wild ones like boars) and birds were killed and its *finale* was marked by the sacrifice of 21 sterile cows,[28] though the *Taittiriya Samhita* (V.6.11-20) enumerates only 180 animals including horses, bulls, cows, goats, deer, nilgais to be killed.[29] The *gosava* (cow sacrifice) was an important component of the *rajasuya* and *vajapeya* sacrifices. In the latter, the *Shatapatha Brahmana* tells us, a sterile spotted cow was offered to Maruts.[30] Similarly in the *agnishtoma* a sterile cow was sacrificed.[31] According to the *Taittiriya*

Brahmana an important element in the *panchasharadiyasava* was the 'immolation' of seventeen 'dwarf heifers under three'[32] and on the day preceding the sacrifice the sacrificer himself was required to eat the forest plants or fruits.[33] The killing of animals including cattle (*pashu*)[34] figures in several other *yajnas* including *caturmasya*,[35] *sautramani*,[36] and independent animal sacrifice called *pashubandha* or *nirudhapashubandha*,[37] which was also an important component of many sacrifices.

IV

The evidence cited above indicates that cattle were killed not only for sacrifice but also for food. Sacrifice and sustenance went hand in hand as was quite natural in the predominantly pastoral society of the Vedic Aryans. Not surprisingly a passage of the *Taittiriya Brahmana* (III.9.8.3), which unambiguously refers to the ritual killing of the cow, states that the cow 'is verily food' (*atho annam vai gauh*), and praises Agastya for his sacrifice of a hundred bulls.[38] That the sacrificed animal was generally meant for human consumption is evident from several texts especially from a passage of the *Taittiriya Samhita* (VI.3.10.2-6), which tells us about the mode of cutting up the immolated animal and gives an idea of the distribution of its flesh.[39] More explicit is the *Gopatha Brahmana* (Purvabhaga, I.3.18) of the *Atharvaveda* according to which the carcass was to be divided into thirty-six shares by the *samitara* who killed the victim by strangulation. There is thus evidence to show that the flesh of the cattle slaughtered in public sacrifices was consumed by various categories of people. It is significant that out of 250 animals mentioned in the Vedas 50 were considered fit for sacrifice and for eating.[40]

V

There is substantial evidence to show that killing of cattle and other animals was not restricted to public sacrifices; it was, in fact, *de rigueur* in ordinary and day-to-day domestic rites and rituals as well. Among the rites relating to agriculture, which tended to become stable from the later Vedic period onwards, mention may be made of the *shulagava* (sacrifice of 'the ox on the spit') referred to by several Grihyasutras.[41] In this sacrifice a spit-ox was killed for Rudra; its tail and skin, etc., were thrown into the fire and its blood was poured out on the *kusha* or *darbha* grass for the snakes.[42] The emergence of sedentary agriculture led to the growth of fixed settlements, which provided the context for the formulation of detailed and often complicated rules relating to the construction and occupation of houses (*vastu-pratishtha*) found in the texts. Of the many rules at least two provide for the sacrifice of a black cow or white goat.[43]

An interesting rite repeatedly mentioned in the texts from the later Vedic period onwards is the reception of guests and is called *arghya*, or more popularly, *madhuparka*. The killing of the kine to honour guests seems to have been prevalent from earlier times. The *Rigveda* mentions the word *atithinir*,[44] which has been interpreted as 'cows fit for guests',[45] and refers to a Vedic hero, Atithigva whose name literally means 'slaying cows for guests'.[46] It also refers to the killing of cow on festive occasions like marriage[47] but the word *madhuparka*, is first referred to by the *Jaiminiya Upanishad-Brahmana* (I.59.3) and discussed at length in several Grihyasutras.[48] It was performed in honour of special guests, namely the teacher, the priest, a *snataka*, father-in-law, paternal and maternal uncles, a friend and a king. Their reception not only included the offering of a mixture of curd and honey (whence the term *madhuparka* was derived) but, more importantly, of a cow which was either immolated[49] or let loose according to their wishes, though in no case the rite was performed without beef or flesh-meat. Several Grihyasutras describe *madhuparka* both independently[50] as well as part of the marriage ceremonies in which cow was slain more than once in honour of guests.[51] In subsequent times Panini, therefore, uses the term *goghna* for a guest.[52]

The Grihyasutras also attest to the use of the hide of the bull or the cow in domestic rituals like the *simantonnayana* (lit. parting of the hair ceremony performed in the fourth month of pregnancy) and the *upanayana* (investiture ceremony preceding the beginning of one's studenthood) implying cattle killing.[53] Cattle, in fact, seem to have been killed even on what would appear to be a flimsy ground to many of us. Thus if one were eager to have a learned son with a long life he could find solution in the Upanishadic precept which permitted such a person to eat a mess of veal or beef or of other flesh with rice and *ghee*.[54]

The practice of cattle killing was also intimately connected with the cult of the dead, which occupies considerable space in the Vedic as well as post-Vedic texts. One of the Rigvedic passages (X.16.7ab) relating to cremation, for example, refers to the use of the skin and the thick fat of the cow to cover the dead body, and the *Atharvaveda* (XII.2, 48) speaks of a bull 'presumably being burnt along with the dead to ride with in the next world'. The Grihyasutras, elaborately describing the funerary procedure, provide ample evidence of cattle killing at the time of cremation and of the practice of distributing different limbs of the animal on those of the corpse.[55] The cremation was followed by several rites performed in honour of the Manes, variously mentioned as *pitriyajna*, *mahapitriyajna* and *ashtaka* in the Vedic passages and as some other types of *shraddha* discussed in the post-Vedic texts, especially the Grihyasutras.[56] The purpose of the different types of *shraddha* was to satisfy the Manes by feeding them well. But this could be possible only if beef was offered to them and hence, in addition to other animals, cows and/or bulls were slain for them.[57]

One of the *shraddhas* called *abhyudayika* was performed to please the Manes as a preliminary to such festive occasions as the birth of a son and the marriage of the son or daughter. In another type of *shraddha* called the *ashtaka* or the *ekashtaka*, of which the Grihyasutras[58] speak at length, the killing of cow is explicitly referred to. The performer of the *ashtaka* rite, we are told, prepared the cow for immolation and offered its cooked omentum to the Manes,[59] though the degree of satisfaction they derived from the *shraddha* seems to have varied sometimes according to the animal offered. For, we are told, the flesh of the cow gratified the *pitris* (dead ancestors) for a year (*samvatsaram gavyena pritih*), that of the buffalo, wild animals (e.g. hares) and domesticated (i.e. village) animals like goats for more than a year and the Manes remained satisfied for an endless period of time if the flesh of rhinoceros, *shatabali* (a kind of fish) and *varddhrinasa* was offered to them.[60] However not everything depended on the choice of the Manes and preference for beef was generally unquestioned. After all, the *shraddha*, apart from being a ritual to please the ancestors, was also a feast for the community members, especially the brahmins, whose craving for beef is clearly indicated in the texts.

Like the *shraddha*, there were other occasions when cattle were slaughtered for the community. The *gavamayana*, a sessional sacrifice performed by the brahmins, was, for example, marked by animal slaughter. It culminated in an extravagant frolicsome festival, *mahavrata*, in which three barren cows were offered to Mitravaruna and other deities,[61] though going by its bacchanalian nature it seems likely that many more cattle were slaughtered. Similarly the *grihamedha,* which has been discussed in several Shrautasutras,[62] was some kind of a lavish communal feast in which an unspecified number of cows were slain not in the strict ritual manner but in the crude and profane manner.[63] Evidently then, judging by the copious textual references, there is little doubt that the Vedic people slaughtered animals and cattle including the cow whose flesh they ate with great relish. Not surprisingly, beef was the favourite food of Yajnavalkya, the much respected sage from Mithila, who famously said that he would continue to eat the flesh of cows and oxen so long as it was tender (*amsala*).[64] His obdurate position may imply that already in his time the opinion against beef eating was surfacing in society.

VI

The practice of killing cattle including the cow is amply attested by archaeological material dispersed widely over time and space. We have it on the authority of India's topmost archaeologist, the late H.D. Sankalia, that throughout the pleistocene period ranging from about a hundred thousand to ten thousand years 'bones of the cow/ox have been discovered more frequently and at a large number of places in the river and other deposits than of any other animal'.[65] Found in association with stone tools, these bones indicate that the primitive man hunted them for food. But even when man in India reached a civilized stage, he continued to kill animals to meet his dietary requirements. Excavations clearly prove that the authors of the Harappan civilization ate cattle flesh of which the relevant archaeological evidence is spread over a vast area covering Sindh, Punjab, Uttar Pradesh, Rajasthan, Kutch, Saurashtra and coastal Gujarat. Outside the Harappan cultural zone there is ample faunal evidence indicative of the Chalcolithic dietary culture marked by the practice of eating cattle flesh.[66] Archaeological evidence also testifies to the continuation of this practice throughout the Vedic period and even later. Excavations carried out at many places identified by archaeologists as the Painted Grey Ware sites, whose cultural assemblage mostly belongs to the later Vedic phase when the Aryan settlements became stable in the Indo-Gangetic divide, are very clear on the point. At Hastinapur (Meerut district), for example, the bones of buffalo, sheep, goat, pig, elephant, and, most importantly, of cattle resembling the smaller, humpless, short-horned variety of today, have been found. A substantial number of them range in date from the eleventh century to roughly the third century BC. Many bone fragments of cattle are either charred or bear definite cut marks, which suggests that these animals were slaughtered for food.[67] At Allahpur (Meerut district), where a later Vedic settlement was excavated, charred bones along with horns were found.[68] Similar evidence is much more impressive from Atranjikhera (Etah district) where the total number of identified bone fragments goes to 927. Of these more than 64 per cent accounts for the bones of cow, often with cut marks and predates fifth century BC. Beef, thus, appears to have been a favoured item of food, though other types of meat were also consumed. At Bhagwanpura in Haryana, a large number of charred bones of cattle have been found.[69] At Ropar (600-200 BC) in Punjab, the later phase of the Painted Gray Ware settlement has yielded bones of domesticated cattle, buffalo, sheep, goat, pig, horse, dog, fowl, tortoise and chital with cut marks and signs of charring, implying their use to meet the dietary needs of the people.[70] Interestingly, evidence of cattle killing also comes from the second phase of human habitation (*c.* 400-200 BC) at Mathura whose association with the cattle protector Krishna is well known.[71] In fact, of all the osteological remains cattle bones are the most common at the PGW sites excavated so far and this leads us to the unmistakable conclusion that cattle domestication was linked with dietary as well as non-dietary economic uses. The Vedic textual references to cattle flesh as an important dietary item, thus, tie up well with archaeological evidence.

VII

Despite the massive evidence of cattle killing and beef eating in the Vedic period, many scholars, especially those of Hindutva persuasion, have argued that the cow was sacred and unslayable. They have relied solely on the occurrence of the word *aghnya* (not to be slain) for the cow in the Vedic texts. But the term *aghnya/aghnyā* (lit. not to be slain) has been used at four places in the *Rigveda* and the *Atharvaveda* 'as a masculine noun equivalent to bull or ox and 42 times with a feminine ending to mean a cow'.[72] Attention has also been drawn to the use of words for cow as epithet or in simile and metaphor with reference to entities of highest religious significance,[73] though these occurrences do not indicate their primary sense with reference to the actual animal. Neither of the two types of evidence adduced in favour of the 'sacredness' of the Vedic cow indicates that it was 'sacred' and unslayable. If anything, the Vedic evidence may imply the economic importance of the cows as can be inferred from their various uses.[74] When slaughtered the cows provided food to the people and their priests. When milked they gave additional nourishment not only through milk but also through a variety of dairy products, which formed part of human diet as well as of the Vedic sacrificial oblation (*havis*). They produced oxen, which were used as draught animals. The cattle hide was used in a variety of ways. The bowstring (*jya*) was made of a thong of cowhide – a practice that may have continued in later times.[75] The different parts of the chariot were tied together with leather straps, which were also needed for binding the arrow to the shaft. The goad for driving the animals was made of cow's skin or tail. Leather strings were used not only for making snares but also a kind of musical instrument called *godha*.[76] The utility and importance of the cattle therefore inspired warriors to fight wars (*gavishti*) for them and it is likely that part of the cattle stock of the vanquished tribes was killed in course of the raids. All this goes against the popular notion of the inviolability of the cow in the Vedic period and proves that it was certainly killed for sacrifice (*yajna*) and food as well as for other requirements.

It seems likely, however, that the brahmin's cow was inviolable. It is known that the cow was an ideally preferred form of *dakshina*[77] (sacrificial fee) given to the brahmin priest. There are many references to the Vedic brahmin's interest in his *dakshina* (the good milch cow),[78] and to 'the dire consequences that will befall one who withholds it or injures or misappropriates it and the corresponding benefit accruing to him who bestows it'.[79] At one place in the *Atharvaveda* we come across a warning: 'O king (*nripati*), the gods did not give that [cow] to you to eat; O warrior (*rajanya*), do not desire to eat the brahman's cow, [she is] not to be eaten (*anadyam*).'[80] It appears, therefore, that the cow could achieve a certain degree of inviolablity only if it was owned by the brahmin or was given to him as *dakshina*. The special importance attached to the brahmin's cow, however, cannot be stretched to argue that the Vedic cow was inherently sacred and could not be slain.

VIII

Although the sacrificial cattle slaughter faced a major challenge from Buddhism and Jainism in the sixth century BC, which vehemently espoused non-violence (*ahimsa*), this did not lead to the disappearance of cattle flesh or other meat types from the Indian dietary menu. Gautama Buddha himself is known to have eaten beef and pork and the texts amply indicate that flesh meat very well suited the Buddhist palate. Ashoka, whose compassion for animals is undeniable, allowed certain specified animals to be killed for his kitchen. But he did not exempt the cow from slaughter. Nor did Kautilya mention cow as unslayable. On the contrary, in his *Arthashastra* he devotes a section each to the superintendents of slaughter house (*sunadhyaksha*)[81] and the cows (*goadhyaksha*);[82] he also makes specific mention of a category of cattle that were fit only for the supply of flesh.[83] There is thus strong evidence to show that cattle were killed for food throughout the Mauryan period.

Like Buddhism, Jainism also enthusiastically took up

cudgels for non-violence and meat eating became a much stronger taboo among its adherents. The inflexibility of the Jaina attitude to animal food is deeply rooted in the basic tenets of Jaina philosophy, which, at least in theory, is impartial in its respect for all forms of life without according any special status to the cow. Thus, although both Buddhism, and Jainism contributed to the growth of *ahimsa* doctrine, neither seems to have developed the notion that the cow was sacred and unslayable.

IX

The practice of ritual and random killing of animals including the cattle continued even in the post-Mauryan centuries as is evident from the legal texts, epics and other literary works. Like the authors of the Dharmasutras, most of which belong to the pre-Mauryan period, Manu, whose law-code (200 BC–AD 200) belongs to the early centuries before and after Christ and is the most representative of the legal texts, has much to say on the lawful and forbidden food. Like them, he allows the consumption of the flesh, among others, of all the domestic animals with teeth in one jaw. He excludes the camel from the list of edible animals but not the cow;[84] nor does he say that this animal is edible. He asserts that animals were created for the sake of sacrifice, that killing on ritual occasions is non-killing[85] and that injury (*himsa*) as enjoined by the Veda (*vedavihitahimsa*) is known to be non-injury.[86] In the section dealing with rules for times of distress, Manu also recalls the legendary examples of the most virtuous brahmins of the days of yore who ate ox-meat and dog-meat to escape death from starvation.[87] It is curious that he does not mention beef as a taboo and permits meat eating on occasions like the *madhuparka* and *shraddha,* etc., without making a specific mention of the bovine meat. This creates some amount of confusion about his position vis-à-vis beef eating, though his commentator Medhatithi (ninth century) clarifies that cow killing on these ritual occasions was an approved Vedic practice.[88]

Like Manu, the lawgiver Yajnavalkya (AD 100-300) discusses the rules regarding lawful and forbidden food. Although his treatment of the subject is less detailed, he does not differ radically from Manu. Yajnavalkya mentions the animals and birds whose flesh could satisfy the Manes.[89] He lays down that a student, teacher, king, close friend and son-in-law should be offered *arghya* every year and a priest should be offered *madhuparka* on all ritual occasions.[90] He further enjoins that a learned brahmin (*shrotriya*) should be welcomed with a big ox or goat, delicious food and sweet words.[91] It would be, however, unrealistic to assume that the dharmic precept of restricting animal slaughter to ritual occasions was always taken seriously either by brahmins for whom the legal injunctions were meant or by other sections of society.[92] For whether or not Yajnavalkya and other lawgivers specifically mention the cow as edible, they generally accept as lawful all those sacrifices, which, according to them, have Vedic sanction. This may have given a *carte blanche* to those who wanted to slaughter animals and domestic bovines during the early Christian centuries and even well into the first millennium AD.

The ambivalence of the post-Mauryan legal texts, however, is absent in the epics. Several characters in the *Mahabharata* are meat eaters; the text even makes a laudatory reference to the king Rantideva in whose kitchen two thousand cows were butchered everyday, and their flesh, along with grains, was distributed among the brahmins.[93] Similarly the *Ramayana* of Valmiki makes reference to the killing of animals including the cow for sacrifice as well as food. Rama was born after his father Dasharatha performed a big sacrifice involving the slaughter of a large number of animals declared edible by the Dharmashastras, which sanction ritual killing of the kine. Sita, while crossing the Yamuna River, assures her that she would worship her with thousand cows and a hundred jars of wine when Rama redeems his vow.[94] She herself seems to be specially fond of deer meat which drives her husband crazy enough to kill Maricha disguised as a fabulous golden deer. Bharadvaja welcomes Rama by slaughtering a fatted calf in his honour.[95]

The non-vegetarian dietary practices are also mentioned in the early Indian medical treatises of Charaka, Sushruta and Vagbhatta; the chronology of the first two broadly coincides with that of the law books of Manu and Yajnavalkya, and the epics, and the third belongs to the seventh century. These texts mention a variety of fish and flesh and refer to the therapeutic uses of beef.[96]

The continuity of the tradition of eating cattle flesh is echoed in early Indian secular literature till late times. In the Gupta period, Kalidasa alludes to the story of Rantideva who killed numerous cows every day in his kitchen,[97] and Varahmihira recommends to a monarch the ceremonial eating of the flesh of several animals including the bull and buffalo.[98] In the post-Gupta centuries several texts refer to cow killing. Bhavabhuti (AD 700) refers to two instances of guest reception, which included the killing of a heifer.[99] Rajashekhara (tenth century) mentions the practice of killing an ox or a goat in honour of a guest[100] and Somadeva (eleventh century) narrates the story of seven brahmin boys who ate a cow.[101] In the twelfth century Shriharsha mentions a variety of non-vegetarian delicacies served at a dazzling marriage feast and refers to two interesting instances of cow killing,[102] though, in the same century the Chalukya King Someshvara shows clear preference for pig flesh over other meat types.

X

It appears from the above survey that unlike the Vedic and post-Vedic texts (Dharmasutras and Grihyasutras), the post-Mauryan sources like the Smritis, epics and the secular literature provide much less evidence of the slaughter of cattle for sacrifice or food. This may imply that the earlier dietary regimen underwent much change over the centuries, and beef eating gradually tended to fall into desuetude. It is not possible to suggest when precisely in the first millennium AD beef disappeared from the brahminical food menu but one can speculate what may have led the people to gradually give up cattle killing.

One of the factors that may have led to the discouragement of sacrificial slaughter of animals may be attributed to the changes in the Vedic religion. Animal sacrifice, which was central to it, was fiercely questioned by the heterodox religions, Buddhism and Jainism, which had a significant impact on the life, culture and the thought of the people. Both the religions gave a boost to the idea of non-kiling of cattle and other animals. Also this idea was gaining ground within the brahminical tradition itself right from the beginning. Already in the *Rigveda* a cow was the symbol of riches and it was likened with Aditi ('mother of gods' but lit. 'boundless heaven'), [103] and the text says : 'don't kill the innocent cow, the Aditi' (8.10.15).[104] Similarly several other Rigvedic passages hint at the need to find substitutes for cattle to be killed in sacrifice.[105] At one place it is stated that 'a devout offering of praise or of fuel stick or of food was as good as a more solemn sacrifice'; at another, we are told that 'oblations of food to the accompaniment of heart-felt hymns become like bulls, oxen and cows in sacrifice. The idea of non-killing of cattle received further support from the later and post-Vedic texts which recommend the offering of animal effigies (*pishtapashu*) in lieu of livestock; for according to them even the offering of rice and barley was equal to an animal sacrifice.

The practice of ritual substitution seems to have been endorsed by some Brahmana texts according to which one who eats the animal in this world would himself be eaten by it in the other world.[106] Such idea was rooted in the theory of *karma* and transmigration often referred to in the Brahmanas and Upanishads according to which the acts committed in this life determined the man's place in the next. The Upanishads questioned the efficacy of animal sacrifice and gave primacy to asceticism as a means of achieving self-realization; they read new meanings in the sacrifices, and buttressed the notion of *ahimsa.*[107]

The gradual shift away from cow killing can also be seen against the background of the transformation of the rural society due to an unprecedented agrarian expansion and the first ever codification of agricultural knowledge in early medieval India.[108] The process of agricultural expansion, triggered by the growing practice of donating land and other agrarian resources including the cattle to brahmins around the middle of the first millennium led to the recognition of the increasing importance of animal husbandry and to the very negation of the pastoral basis of the Vedic ritualism. Not surprisingly the Puranic texts devote much attention to the new kind of ritual formations of which *dana*, *mahadana*, *tirthas* (pilgrimage), temple worship and *deva puja*, etc., become salient features. All these changes in the socio-cultural and religious spheres coincided with the growth of the idea of *kaliyuga* which, according to the law books, called for the giving up of many age-old practices, including the killing of kine.[109]

The disapproval of killing cattle in the *kaliyuga*, repeatedly mentioned in the legal texts as a *kalivarjya* (practice forbidden in the Kali age) tended to give a special status to the cow and to exclude beef from the brahminical *carte du jour*. The *Vyasasmriti* (I.12), an early medieval legal text, categorically states that a cow killer is untouchable (*antyaja*), and even by talking to him one incurs sin; it thus made beef eating a basis of untouchability from the early medieval period onwards. Parashara, whose law book is believed to be especially applicable to the *kaliyuga*, lays down that a brahmin who eats beef is required to perform the *kricchrachandrayana* penance (XI.1) and adds that one who kills a cow and hides his offence goes to the worst hell (IX.61-2). The law book of Devala (verse 17) avers that if a brahmin is forced by the *mlecchas*, *chandalas* and the *dasyus* to kill a cow he is required to perform a penance. Like him, many later Smritis condemn cow killing;[110] thus the practice, which they tabooed for the brahmins, came to be increasingly associated with the untouchable castes whose number proliferated over time.

XI

The transformation of the brahminical *haute cuisine* into the daily dietary requirement of the untouchables was the result of a long drawn process and needs to be studied separately against the background of the major social and ideological changes in early India. What, however, is intriguing is that the religious and juridical texts, did not consider cow killing a major offence, despite their strong disapproval of it. In his explanation of a Rigvedic passage (X.5.6), Yaska (*c.* 600 BC), the author of the *Nirukta* and the earliest commentator of the Vedic texts, provides a list of seven sins in which cattle killing does not figure; nor is it mentioned as such in the Brahmanas and the Upanishads. When it begins to figure as a sin from the post-Vedic period onwards, in the Dharmasutras and subsequent legal texts, it does not appear as a *mahapataka* (major sin) but as an *upapataka* (minor sin).[111] It is also curious that the normative literature does not prescribe any physical punishment for the cow killer; it only lays down penances, often elaborate ones, as is seen in the law books of Manu (XI.108-16) and Yajnavalkya (III.263-4) and others. In every case, however, the Smritis provide easy escape routes for intentional as well as inadvertent killing of the cow; sometimes mere feeding of the brahmins could be good enough expiation for the sin.

Another baffling aspect of the Indian cow is that its products played a purificatory role in society from the very beginning, even when the brahmins delighted in beef eating during the Vedic period. The Vedic texts attest to the ritual use of cow's milk and milk products, but in the course of time the mixture of cow products – milk, cow urine and cow dung, curds, and ghee (*panchagavya*) – find frequent mention as purificants in the Dharmashastras. The commentaries and religious digests, most of which belong to the medieval period, abound in references to the *panchagavya* as a purificant, but, they forbid its use by women and shudras; the latter went to hell if they drank it.[112] So deeply were patriarchy and caste discrimination entrenched in society!

Yet another puzzling aspect of the cow is that the prescriptive texts, which repeatedly refer to its purificatory role, also attribute pollution and impurity to this animal. According to Manu the food smelt by the cow has to be purified. Yajnavalkya unambiguously says that while the mouth of the goat and horse is pure that of the cow is not.[113] Among the later juridical texts, those of Angirasa, Parashara, Vyasa and so on, support the idea of impurity of the cow's mouth. The lawgiver Shankha categorically states that all limbs of the cow are pure except her mouth. The commentaries on different Dharmashastra texts reinforce the notion of uncleanliness of the mouth of the cow. All this runs counter to the idea of the purity of the cow and adds to the paradoxes of the cow conundrum.

XII

The brahminical sentiment against cow slaughter continued to gain in strength, and during the medieval period, with the coming of Islam, it became quite strong because beef was not a taboo among its followers.[114] Cow killing may have been the cause of occasional Hindu-Muslim tension and efforts may have been made to ease it. For example, Damodara, the elder brother of Nilakantha (seventeenth century?), is said to have persuaded the *yavanas* of Mulasthana (Multan) to give up cow slaughter.[115] But this may have been an isolated case of friendly persuasion; for at least two clashes over the cow issue in the seventeenth and eighteenth centuries are documented.[116] Thus while in the pre-Islamic period beef eating caused a social contradiction between the brahmins and untouchables, now it became the basis of religious antagonism between Hindus and Muslims. It is an irony that the brahmins who may have 'fattened' themselves on beef during Vedic times now stereotyped Muslims as beef eaters!

It may have been in response to the occasional conflict over the cow issue that Akbar (AD 1556-1605), under the influence of Jains, especially Harivijaya Suri and Vijaysen Suri, adopted the policy of issuing *firmans* on different occasions ordering his officials not to allow the slaughter of animals (including the cow); the policy was followed by his successor Jahangir (AD 1605-27) as well. Obviously both were trying to control inter-religious tensions. Even the much talked about Humayun's will which advised Babur not to allow the killing of cows was possibly a response to the views of the brahmins. Although the will itself was a later forgery, perhaps of the eighteenth century, it does indicate the state's willingness to respect the view that was gaining ground among them.

While the cow was emerging as an emotive cultural symbol in the brahminical circles during the medieval period, it became more emotive with the rise of the Maratha power in the seventeenth century under Shivaji (AD 1627-80), who was often viewed as an incarnation of god who descended on earth for the deliverance of the cow and the brahmin. But it was first used for mass political mobilization by the Sikh Kuka (Namdhari) movement, which rallied Hindus and Sikhs against the British, who had allowed the killing of cows in the Punjab. At around the same time, Dayananda Saraswati founded the first Gorakshini Sabha in 1882. He made the cow a symbol of the unity of a wide range of people against Muslims and challenged their practice of its slaughter, provoking a series of Hindu-Muslim riots in the 1880s, 1890s and the early years of the twentieth century. With the intensification of the cow-protection movement the cow became the mother, *gaumata*,[117] more or less at the time when Bharat emerged as *Bharat Mata*; the recently invented Rashtramata (Padmavati) is a latecomer on the scene. But together they are debasing the cultural and political discourse in the country.[118]

XIII

The history of the cow is thus riddled with puzzles and paradoxes. In Vedic and post-Vedic periods, when the ritual or non-ritual killing of this animal and eating its flesh was very much in vogue, it was considered to be an item of wealth and was likened with Aditi (mother of gods). In subsequent times, if it was killed according to Vedic precepts, it was not killing, because Vedic killing was not killing. Even when the slaughter of bovines came to be forbidden in the Kali age, cow-killing remained only a minor sin for which no corporal punishment was meted out to the offender; he could atone for his sin by observing some penances, often as light as satisfying the brahminical gluttony. When the Dharmashastras assigned a purificatory role to the five products of the cow, they considered its faeces and urine as pure but not its mouth; and food smelt by it needed to be purified. As long as the brahmins continued to eat cow meat it remained a delicacy and when they gave it up, it was banished to the polluted culinary world of the untouchables. With the advent of Islam, the Hindus treated cow-killing its 'baneful bequeathal' to India despite the long history of ritual butchery of cattle by their own ancestors, and stereotyped the Muslims as beef eaters who supposedly posed a serious threat to the elusive 'Hindu' identity. It is through these incongruous attitudes that the Indian cow has struggled its way to sanctity. But how it has continued to vitiate the social and political discourse in India is beyond the scope of present enquiry.

NOTES

1. *Indo-Aryans*, Calcutta, 1891, vol. 1, chapter VI.
2. H.D. Sankalia, '(The Cow) in History', *Seminar*, no. 93, May 1967.
3. Laxman Shastri Joshi, 'Was the Cow Killed in Ancient India?', *Quest*, 75 (March-April 1972), pp. 83-7.
4. R.S. Sharma, *Material Culture and Social Formations in Ancient India*, Delhi, 1983, p. 24.
5. Doris Srinivasan, *Concept of Cow in the Rigveda,* Delhi, 1979, p. 1.
6. R.S. Sharma, *Looking for the Aryans*, Chennai, 1994, p. 42.
7. *The Zend Avesta*, Sacred Books of the East, XXIII, pt. 2, pp. 62-6, 79; ibid., Sacred Books of the East, IV, pp. 232-3.
8. *Rigveda* (hereafter *RV*) X. 86.14ab.
9. *RV*, X.28.3c.
10. *RV*, X.27.2c.
11. *RV*, VI.17.11b.
12. *RV*, V.29.7ab.
13. *RV*, VIII.12.8ab.
14. A. B. Keith, *The Religion and Philosophy of the Veda and Upanishads,* Harvard Oriental Series, 1925, Indian reprint, Delhi, 1970, p. 154.
15. *RV*, VIII.43.11 cited in P.V. Kane, *History of Dharmashastra*, II, pt. 2, Poona, 1974, p. 772, fn. 1847.
16. Harry Falk, 'Zur Tierzucht Im Alten Indien', *Indo-Iranian Journal*, 24 (1982), p. 176.
17. Srinivasan (op. cit., pp. 58-60) thinks that only the barren cow (*vasa*) was sacrificed which is the consensus among scholars. But according to Stephanie W. Jamison the *vasa* is a cow (or other female domestic animal) that has been bred but has not calved (*The Ravenous Hyenas and the Wounded Sun*, Ithaca, 1991, pp. 258-9).
18. *RV*, X.91.14ab. Also see Rajnikant Shastri, *Hindu Jati ka Utthan aur Patan,* Allahabad, 1988, pp. 101-2.
19. *RV*, X.16.4ab; X.16.7ab. Also see Keith, op. cit., p. 419.
20. For divergent views on the birth and attributes of Soma see A.A. Macdonell, *Vedic Mythology*, Strassburg, 1897, Indian reprint,

Varanasi, 1963, pp. 102-14. Cf. Harry Falk, 'Soma I and II', *Bullettin of the School of Oriental and African Studies,* 52, pt. 1 (1989), pp. 77-90; Asko Parpola, 'The Problem of the Aryans and the Soma: Textual-linguistic and Archaeological Evidence', in George Erdosy, ed., *The Indo-Aryans of South Asia,* Delhi, 177; Harri Nyberg, 'The Problem of the Aryans and the Soma: The Botanical Evidence', ibid.

21. Louis Renou, *Vedic India,* Indian reprint, Varanasi, 1971, p. 104.
22. Keith, op. cit., p. 327.
23. Ibid., p. 87. Teetotalism was unknown to the Vedic gods and Indra, pot bellied from excessive drinking, is said to have drunk three lakes of *soma* before slaying the dragon Vritra. Macdonell, op. cit., p. 56.
24. G.U. Thite, *Sacrifice in the Brahmana Texts,* Poona, 1975, chapter VI.
25. Sharma, *Material Culture,* op. cit., p. 119. Cf. Keith, op. cit., pp. 324-6.
26. Renou, op. cit., p. 102.
27. In *RV,* I.162, 163, the details of the horse sacrifice are available for the first time.
28. Renou, op. cit., p. 109.
29. *Taittiriya Samhita* (hereafter *TS*), V.6.11-20. Also see Sayana's commentary on *Taittiriya Brahmana* (hereafter *TB*), III.9.1.1. cited by R. L. Mitra, *Indo-Aryans: Contributions to the Elucidation of Ancient and Mediaeval History,* rpt., Varanasi, 1969, vol. 1, p. 362). Cf. *TS,* III.8-9 and various passages in the *Shatapatha Brahmana* (hereafter *SB*), XIII, *TS,* V, and *TB,* III.
30. Thite, op. cit., p. 77.
31. Renou, op. cit., 105; Kane, op. cit., II, pt. 2, pp. 1158, 1200-1 also draws attention to a passage which says that instead of the cow a bull or only *payasya* may be offered to Mitra and Varuna.
32. Mitra, op. cit., p. 363.
33. *SB,* I.1.1.9-10, cited in Thite, op. cit., p. 193.
34. Monier Monier-Williams, *Sanskrit-English Dictionary, s.v. pashu.* Cf. Macdonell and Keith, *Vedic Index,* I, pp. 580-2. The Sanskrit *pashu* = Avestan *pasu* means domestic animals, livestock and sacrificial animals but it also frequently indicates simply cattle as the domestic animal and the sacrificial animal par excellence,

Bruce Lincoln, *Priests, Warriors and Cattle*, p. 65 and fn. 98. Mayrhofer, *A Concise Etymological Dictionary*, II, pp. 239-40, *s.v. pashuh*.

35. Keith, op. cit., p. 323; J.C. Heesterman, *The Ancient Indian Royal Consecration*, The Hague, 1957, p. 28.
36. Kane, op. cit., II, pt. 2, p. 1224; for details see ibid., chapter, XXXV; Thite, op. cit., pp. 83-9. Also see 'animal' in the index to M.B. Kolhatkar, *Sura: The Liquor and the Vedic Sacrifice*, Delhi, 1999.
37. Keith, op. cit., p. 324; Kane (op. cit., II, pt. 2, chapter XXXII) discusses the details of the sacrifice on the basis of *SB*, *TS*, and several Sutra texts belonging to the post-Vedic period.
38. K.T. Achaya, *A Historical Dictionary of Indian Food*, Delhi, 1999, p. 145.
39. For a detailed discussion see Mitra, op. cit., pp. 373-4.
40. K.T. Achaya, *A Historical Dictionary of Indian Food*, p. 145. It is, however, stated at some places that the flesh of animals like dogs was thrown to demons. The entrails of a dog were cooked in a situation of extreme destitution (*avartya suna antrani pece*, *RV*, IV.18.13a). In the post-Vedic period the notion of impurity of the flesh of several other animals figures in the Sutra literature (Om Prakash, *Food and Drinks in Ancient India,* Delhi, 1961, pp. 39-40).
41. Renou, op. cit., p. 114; Mitra (op. cit., pp. 363 ff.) has interpreted *shulagava* as a sacrifice of 'spitted ox' or roast beef. The word *shula* is found in the *Rigveda* only once, but it occurs more often in the later Brahmanas (Renou, op. cit., p. 114; Mitra, op. cit., pp. 363 ff.). Cf. Kane, op. cit., II, pt. 2, pp. 831-2; J. Gonda, *Vedic Ritual: The Non-Solemn Rites*, Leiden, 1980, pp. 435-7.
42. Keith, op. cit., p. 364.
43. V.M. Apte (*Social and Religious Life in the Grhyasutras*, Bombay, 1939, p. 144) points out that of the various Grihyasutra texts only those of Gobhila and Khadira prescribe an animal sacrifice for *Vastospati* on the completion of house construction.
44. *RV*, X.68.3.
45. Herman W. Tull, 'The Killing That is not Killing: Men, Cattle and the Origins of Non-Violence (*Ahimsa*) in the Vedic Sacrifice', *Indo-Iranian Journal*, 39 (1996), 229. Cf. Manfred Mayrhoffer,

Etymologisches Worterbuch des Altindoarischen, Heideberg, 1986, vol. I, p. 57, s.v. *atithi*.

46. Macdonell & Keith, op. cit., II, p. 145. Also see Kane, op. cit., II, pt. 2, pp. 749-56. The epithet Atithigva is also often used for the Rigvedic chief Divodasa and has been interpreted by Bloomfield as 'he who (always) has a cow for a guest' (*Journal of American Oriental Society*), 16, 1894, p. cxxiv.
47. *RV*, X.85.13c.
48. For references see Kane, op. cit., II, pt. 1, chapter X; Ram Gopal, *India of Vedic Kalpasutras*, Delhi, 1959, pp. 456-8; Mitra, op. cit., pp. 379-83; Keith, op. cit., p. 363; Apte, op. cit., p. 230.
49. Shingo Einoo has provided a very useful table showing the procedures of *madhuparka* and indicating the specific Sutra passages which refer to the killing of cow in honour of guests: Einoo, 'The Formation of the Puja Ceremony', in Hanns-Peter Schmidt and Albrecht Wezler, eds., *Veda-Vyakarana-Vyakhyana: Festschrift Paul Thieme zum 90,* Reinbek, 1996, pp. 83-4.
50. D.N. Jha, *The Myth of the Holy Cow*, London, 2002, p. 51, nn. 71, 72 and 73.
51. Ibid., p. 33.
52. *Ashtadhyayi*, 3.4.73; V.S. Agrawala, *India as Known to Panini*, Varanasi, 2nd edn., 1963, p. 100.
53. Jha, op. cit., pp. 33-4.
54. *Brihadaranyaka Upanishad*, VI. 4. 18: *The Principal Upanishads* (with introduction, text and translation), ed. S. Radhakrishnan, Centenary Edition, 4th Impression, Delhi, 1991, p. 326.
55. Ram Gopal, op. cit., pp. 360-1; Kane, op. cit., IV, pp. 189-266. The animal killed at the time of cremation was called *anustarani* which according to Kane (ibid., p. 206, fn. 486) means either a cow or a she-goat. But V.S. Apte interprets it as a cow sacrificed at the funeral ceremony (*The Practical Sanskrit-English Dictionary*, s.v. *anustaranam*). A suggestion has also been made that the *anustarani* cow is 'normally one that has not calved' (W. Norman Brown, 'The Sanctity of the Cow in Hinduism', *Madras University Journal*, XXVIII, no. 2, 1957, p. 33, fn. 17).
56. The word *shraddha* is not found in the Vedic texts and, according to Kane (op. cit., IV, p. 350), it first occurs in the *Kathopanishad* (1.3.17). But it comes to occupy a very important place in the

Dharmashastra literature and more than fifteen specialized treatises devoted to the procedures of *shraddha* were produced in medieval times.

57. According to the *Apastamba Grihyasutra* (II.7.16.25) 'the Manes derive great pleasure from the flesh of cow' (Banerji, op. cit., p. 157). According to the *Paraskar Grihyasutra* (III. 10. 48-9), on the eleventh day after the death, the relatives of the dead should feed an odd number of brahmins a meal with meat; it adds that a cow could also be killed in honour of the dead (III.10.48-9).
58. *Hiranyakeshi Grihyasutra*, II.15.1; *Baudhayana Grihyasutra*, II.11.51; *Vaikhanasa Grihyasutra*, IV.3.
59. *Apastamba Grihyasutra*, VIII.22.3-4.
60. Ibid., II.7.16.25; II.7.17.3, cited in Kane, op. cit., IV, p. 422.
61. Kane, ibid., II, pt. 2, p. 1245. The *mahavrata* seems to have been some kind of a folk ritual marked by many bizarre practices. For a discussion of the *gavamayana* and *mahavrata* see ibid., pp. 1239-46; Keith, op. cit., pp. 351-2; Renou, op. cit., p. 107; Jogiraj Basu, *India of the Age of the Brahmanas*, Calcutta, 1969, pp. 162-5; Ram Gopal, op. cit., pp. 169-71; Thite, op. cit., pp. 100-2.
62. J.C Heesterman, *The Broken World of Sacrifice: An Essay in Ancient Indian Ritual,* Chicago, 1993, pp. 190-3, 200-2.
63. Heesterman argues that in the case of *grihamedha*, the word used for cow slaughter is derived from the root han (to kill) which is different from the ritualistic killing indicated in the Vedic sacrifices by the term *alambhana* (op. cit., pp. 189-201).
64. *SB*, III.1.2.21 quoted in Kane, op. cit., II, pt. 2, p. 773. The exact meaning of the word *amsala* is controversial. It has generally been translated as 'tender' but, according to M. Witzel, it might as well mean 'fatty' (Witzel, 'On the Sacredness of the Cow in India' unpublished manuscript, abbreviated version published as Ushi. wo meguru Indojin no kagae (in Japanese), The Association of Humanities and Sciences, Kobe Gakuin University, 1991, no. 1, pp. 9-20.
65. Sankalia, '(The Cow) in History', op. cit., p. 13.
66. H.D. Sankalia, *Prehistory and Protohistory of India and Pakistan,* 2nd edn., Poona, 1974, pp. 461, 484, etc.
67. B.B. Lal, 'Excavations at Hastinapur and Other Explorations in

the Upper Ganga and Satlej Basins', *Ancient India,* nos. 10-11 (1954-5); B. Nath, 'Animal Remains from Hastinapur', *Ancient India*, nos. 10-11 (1954-5), pp. 107-20; B.P. Sahu, *From Hunters to Breeders*, Delhi, 1988, pp. 233-5.

68. Vibha Tripathi, *Painted Grey Ware: An Iron Age Culture of Northern India,* Delhi, 1976, p. 24.
69. Sahu, op. cit., p. 237.
70. B. Nath, 'Animal Remains from Rupar and Bara Sites...', *Indian Museum Bulletin*, III, nos. 1-2, pp. 69-116; Sahu, op. cit., pp. 235-6.
71. A.K. Sharma, 'Faunal Remains from Mathura', in J.P. Joshi et al., eds, *Facets of Indian Civilization – Recent Perspectives: Essays in Honour of Prof. B.B. Lal,* Delhi, 1997, III, p. 824.
72. Brown, op. cit., p. 33. Kane (op. cit., II, pt. 2, pp. 772-3) also cites Vedic passages mentioning the word *aghnya.*
73. Macdonell (op. cit., pp. 150-1) makes the valid point that the cow entered the conceptions of Vedic mythology – a view repeated by him and Keith in the *Vedic Index,* II, p. 146. But on Macdonell's own admission, this was owing to the great utility of the cow.
74. See Srinivasan, op. cit., chapter II.
75. S.D. Singh, *Ancient Indian Warfare with Special Reference to the Vedic Period,* Leiden, 1965, p. 93, fn. 2 and p. 103.
76. Srinivasan, op. cit., p. 14. In our own time cowhide forms a crucial element of the double-headed leather drum called *Mridangam* (S. Anand, 'Thyagraj's Cow', *Outlook,* 8 September 2003).
77. Etymologically the word *dakshina* is so called because it imparts power or strength to the receiver (Apte, *The Practical Sanskrit-English Dictionary, s.v. daksina*). It is used in the sense of a good milch cow or 'the richly milking one' in the Vedic texts because it gave wealth and hence strength to the priest. See Thite, op. cit., pp. 151-61.
78. M. Bloomfield, *Religion of the Veda*, New York, 1908, pp. 69ff.
79. Brown, op. cit., p. 43 draws attention to several passages from the *Rigveda* and the *Atharvaveda* to prove this point. Also see Herman W. Tull, 'The Killing That Is Not Killing: Men, Cattle and the Origins of Non-Violence in the Vedic Sacrifice', *Indo-Iranian Journal*, 39 (1996), pp. 236-7.
80. *AV*, 5.18.1.
81. *Arthashastra* II.26

82. Ibid., II.29.
83. Ibid., II, 29.5.
84. *Manusmriti,* V.18.
85. Ibid., V.39.
86. Ibid., V.44.
87. Ibid., X.105-9.
88. Medhatithi on *Manu*, V.27, 41 see *Manava-Dharma-Shastra*, ed. V.N. Mandalik, Bombay, 1886, pp. 604, 613.
89. *Yajnavalkyasmriti*, I.258-61.
90. Ibid., I.110.
91. *mahoksham va mahajam va shrotriyayopakalpayet,* ibid., I.109.
92. The law giver Brihaspati (AD 300-500), while discussing the importance of local customs, says that in Madhyadesha the artisans eat cows (*madhyadeshe karmakarah shilpinashca gavasinah*), *Brihaspatismriti*, 128b, Gaekwad Oriental Series, Baroda, 1941.
93. *Mahabharata*, III.208.8-9.
94. *Ramayana*, Kumbakonam edition, 2.55.19cd-20ab.
95. Mitra, op. cit., vol. I, p. 396.
96. *Caraka Samhita: Sutrasthanam,* II.31, XXVII.79: *Sushruta Samhita: Sarirasthanam*, III.25; *Astanga Hrdayam: Sutrasthanam*, VI.65.
97. *Meghaduta*, with the commentary of Mallinatha, ed. and tr., M.R. Kale (ed. & tr.), Delhi, 1979, I.48.
98. Ajaya Mitra Shastri, *India as Seen in the Brihatsamhita*, Delhi, 1969, p. 214.
99. *Mahaviracharita*, Rampratap Tripathi Shastri (ed. with Hindi tr.), Allahabad, 1973. III.2. *Uttararamacarita,* with notes and the commentary of Ghanasyama, P.V. Kane and C.N. Joshi (ed. and tr.), Delhi, 1962, Act IV.
100. *Balaramayana*, of Rajashekhara, ed. Gangasagar Rai, Varanasi, 1984, I.38a.
101. *Kathasaritsagara*, VI.117-18.
102. *Naishadhamahakavyam* with the commentary of Mallinatha, Haragovind Shastri (ed.), Varanasi, 1981, XVII.173, 197.
103. Jha, op. cit., p. 38. Michael Witzel, 'On the sacredness of the cow in India', unpublished manuscript. For a fuller discussion of the importance of the cow in economic, ritual and mythological contexts see Srinivasan, *Concept of Cow in the Rigveda*, op. cit.

104. Cited in Witzel, op. cit.
105. *RV*, VIII.19.5; VIII.24.20, cited in Kane, op. cit., II, pt. 2, p. 775. *RV*, VI.16.47, cited in Kane, op. cit., II, pt. 2, p. 775, f. 1854. Also see Brian K. Smith and Wendy Doniger, 'Sacrifice and Substitution: Ritual Mystification and Mythical Demystification', *Numen*, 36, 2, 1989, pp. 189-223.
106. *Kaushitaki Brahmana,* 11.3; *Shatapatha Brahmana,* 12.9.1.1. Hanns Peter Schmidt, 'The Origin of Ahimsa', *Melanges d'Indianisme a la memoire de Louis,* Paris, 1968, pp. 644-5; idem, 'Ahimsa and Rebirth', in Michael Witzel, ed., *Inside the Texts Beyond the Texts*, Harvard Oriental Series, Cambridge, 1997, pp. 214-15; cf. Smith and Doniger, op. cit., pp. 189-224.
107. The word *ahimsa/ ahimsayai* finds mention in several later Vedic and post-Vedic texts. But there is a wide divergence of scholarly opinion on the origin of the idea of non-violence (*ahimsa*). According to Hanns-Peter Schmidt ('The Origin of Ahimsa', op. cit., p. 653) the word *ahimsa* first occurs in the sense of a new doctrine in the teachings of Ghora Angirasa found in *Chhandogya Upanishad* (III.17.4). According to Ludwig Alsdorf (Beitrage zur Geschichte von Vegetarismus und Rinderverehrung in Indien, Weisbaden, 1962) the doctrine of *ahimsa* originated in the Indus Valley civilization and J.C. Heesterman, like Schmidt, locates the origin of the doctrine within the Vedic-brahminical tradition ('Non-Violence and Sacrifice', *Indologica Taurinensia*, XII, 1984, p. 120). As opposed to these scholars Witzel has asserted that the origin of *ahimsa* lies in the horror of killing and in this sense non-violence 'is a selfish action, not altruism and love for all beings ... a prudent action taken in one's own interest ... not necessarily a Jaina, Buddhist, or an "aboriginal" development at all, but one which has its roots in much earlier Brahmanical thought' (Witzel, 'On the Sacredness of the Cow in India', op. cit). There is, however, a strong opinion in favour of the shramana traditions as being the source of *ahimsa* doctrine.
108. That there took place a consolidation of agricultural knowledge during the early medieval and later period is attested by such texts as the *Brihatsamhita*, *Agnipurana*, *Krishiparashara*,

Kashyapiyakrishisukti and *Upavanavinoda* of Sarngadhara (thirteenth century) as well as by the maxims and pithy sayings of Daka and Khana.

109. The number of practices forbidden in the *kaliyuga* increased to more than fifty and came to be consolidated in the seventeeth century by Damodara in his *Kalivarjyavinirnaya*. For a detailed discussion of the development of the idea of *kaliyuga* and its relationship with social and economic transformation see R.S. Sharma, 'The Kali Age: A Period of Social Crisis', in D.N. Jha, ed., *The Feudal Order*, pp. 61-77; B.N.S. Yadava, 'The Accounts of the Kali Age and the Social Transition from Antiquity to the Middle Ages', ibid., pp. 79-120; Jha, op. cit., Editor's Introduction, pp. 6-10.
110. *Atrismriti*, verses 218, 315; *Yamasmriti*, verse 30; *Angirasasmriti*, verse 25-34; *Samvarttasmriti*, verses 132-7, 198; *Parasharasmriti*, IX.36-9. The list of references is illustrative and not exhaustive.
111. S.C. Banerji, *Dharma-Sutras: A Study in their Origin and Development*, Calcutta, 1962, p. 96.
112. *Vishnusmriti,* LIV.7; *Atrismriti*, verses 297, etc.
113 *Manusmriti,* V.125; *Vishnusmriti*, XXIII.38; *Yajnavalkyasmriti*, I.189.
114. Apararka (twelfth century), Devannabhatta (thirteenth century), Madhvacharya (fourteenth century), Madanapala (fourteenth century), Madanaratna (late fifteenth century), Raghunandana (sixteenth century), Nilakantha (seventeenth century), Mitra Mishra (early seventeenth century), and Mahamahopadhyaya Madana Upadhyaya (early twentieth century) categorically reject the idea of cow slaughter in the *kaliyuga*.
115. Kane, op. cit., vol. 1, pt. 2, p. 806.
116. Asim Roy, 'Living Together in Difference: Religious Conflict and Tolerance in pre-Colonial India as History and Discourse', *South Asia: Journal of South Asian Studies*, vol. 33(1), 2010, pp. 45-7.
117. Charu Gupta, 'The Icon of Mother in Late Colonial North India: Bharat Mata, Matri Bhasha and Gau Mata', *Economic and Political Weekly*, 10 November 2001, pp. 4291-9.
118. Recently the Chief Minister of Madhya Pradesh has described Padmavati as Rashtramata and has instituted an award in her name. *The Financial Express*, 21 November 2017.

THREE

Bharatmata: A Short Note on her Long Journey

THE HINDUTVA IDEOLOGUES relentlessly propagate that Bharata, i.e. India, is timeless and it has existed eternally. The first man was born here; and its people were the authors of the first human civilization. They had reached the highest peak of achievement in both the arts and the sciences. The Hindutva fanatics also loudly proclaim that the people of Bharat were conscious of belonging to the Indian nation which they visualized as the mother (Mata). They insist that an Indian can be a nationalist only if he chants Bharatmata ki Jai (Hail Bharatmata) otherwise he should be treated as traitor and anti-national. But to equate parroting of Bharatmata ki Jai with patriotism betrays an abysmal ignorance of history. A critical study of the sources clearly shows that India evolved as a country over a long period and became Bharatmata (Mother India) only in the nineteenth century with the rise of Indian nationalism as a response to Western imperialism.

II

The geographical horizon of the early Aryans, as we know, was limited to the north-western part of the Indian subcontinent, referred to as Saptasindhava,[1] and the word Bharata in the sense of a country is absent from the entire Vedic literature, though the Bharata tribe is mentioned at several places in different contexts. In the *Ashtadhyayi* (IV.2.113) of Panini (500 BC) we find a reference to Prachya Bharata in the sense of a territory (*janapada*) which lay between *Udichya* (north) and *Prachya* (east). It must have been a small region occupied by the Bharatas and cannot be equated with the Akhandabharata of the Hindutva camp. The earliest reference to Bharatavarsha (Prakrit Bharadhavasa) is found in the inscription of Kharavela (first century BC),[2] who lists it among the territories he invaded: but it did not include Magadha, which is mentioned separately in the record. The word may refer here in a general way to northern India, but its precise territorial connotation is vague.

A much larger geographical region is visualized by the use of the word Bharat in the *Mahabharata* (200 BC to AD 300), which provides a good deal of geographical information about the subcontinent, although a large part of the Deccan and the far south does not find any place in it. Among the five divisions of Bharatavarsha named, Madhyadesha finds frequent mention in ancient Indian texts. In the *Amarakosha,* a work of the fourth-fifth centuries, it is used synonymously with Bharata and Aryavarta;[3] the latter, according to its eleventh-century commentator Kshirasvamin, being the same as

Manusmriti's holy land situated between the Himalayas and the Vindhya range (II.22).[4] But in Bana's *Kadambari* (seventh century), at one place Bharatavarsha is said to have been ruled by Tarapida, who 'set his seal on the four oceans' (*dattachatuhsamudramudrah*);[5] and at another, Ujjaini is indicated as being outside Bharatavarsha,[6] which leaves its location far from clear.

Bharatavarsha figures frequently in the Puranas, but they describe its shape variously. In some passages it is likened to a half-moon, in others it is said to resemble a triangle; in yet others it appears as a rhomboid or an unequal quadrilateral or a drawn bow.[7] The *Markandeya Purana* compares the shape of the country with that of a tortoise floating on water and facing east.[8] Most of the Puranas describe Bharatavarsha as being divided into nine *dvipas* or *khandas*, which, being separated by seas, were mutually inaccessible. The Puranic conception of Bharatavarsha has much correspondence with the ideas of ancient Indian astronomers like Varahamihira (sixth century AD) and Bhaskaracharya (eleventh century). However, judging from their identifications of the rivers, mountains, regions and places mentioned in the Puranas, as well as from their rare references to areas south of the Vindhyas, their idea of Bharatavarsha does not seem to have included southern India. Although a few inscriptions of the tenth and eleventh centuries indicate that Kuntala (Karnataka) was situated in the land of Bharata,[9] which is described in a fourteenth-century record as extending from the Himalayas to the southern sea,[10] by and large the available textual and epigraphic references to it do not indicate that the term stood for India as we know it today.

An ambiguous notion of the Bharata region is also found in the *Abhidhanachintamani* of the Jain scholar Hemachandra (twelfth century), who describes it as *karmabhumi* (land of *karma*), as opposed to *phalabhumi* (land of *phala*).[11] He does not clarify what is meant by the two, but his definition of Aryavarta (which may correspond with Bharata) is the same as that found in Manu (IV.14). In fact, Aryavarta figures more frequently than Bharata region in the geohistorical discourses found in early Indian texts. It was only from the 1860s that the name Bharatavarsha, in the sense of the whole subcontinent, found its way into the popular vocabulary.

In many texts Bharata is said to have been a part of Jambudvipa, which itself had an uncertain geographical connotation. The Vedic texts do not mention it; nor does Panini, though he refers to the *jambu* tree (IV.3.165). The Buddhist canonical works provide the earliest reference to the continent called Jambudvipa (Jambudipa in Pali);[12] the name was derived from the *jambu* tree which grew there, having a height of one hundred *yojanas*, a trunk fifteen *yojanas* in girth and outspreading branches fifty *yojanas* in length, whose shade extended to one hundred *yojanas*.[13] It was one of the four *mahadipas* (*mahadvipas*) ruled by a Cakkavatti (Chakravarti). We are told that Buddhas and Cakkavattis were born only in Jambudipa, whose people were more courageous, mindful and religious than the inhabitants of Uttarakuru.[14] Going by the descriptions of Jambudipa and Uttarakuru in the early

Buddhist literature, they both appear to be mythical regions. However, juxtaposed with Sihaladipa (Simhaladvipa = Sri Lanka), Jambudipa stands for India.[15] Ashoka thus uses the word to mean the whole of his empire, which covered nearly the entire Indian subcontinent excluding its far southern part.[16]

But ambiguity about the territorial connotation of Jambudvipa continued during subsequent centuries in both epigraphic and literary sources. In a sixth-century inscription of Toramana, for instance, Jambudvipa occurs without any precise territorial connotation.[17] Similarly, its identification remains uncertain in the Puranic cosmological schema, where it appears more as a mythical region than as a geographical entity. The world, according to the Puranas, 'consists of seven concentric *dvipas* or islands, each of which is encircled by a sea, the central island called Jambudvipa…'.[18] This is similar to the cosmological imaginings of the Jains who, however, placed Jambudvipa at the centre of the central land (*madhyaloka*) of the three-tiered structure of the universe.[19] According to another Puranic conception, which is similar to the Buddhist cosmological ideas, the earth is divided into four *mahadvipas*, Jambudvipa being larger than the others.[20] In both these conceptions of the world, Bharatavarsha is at some places said to be a part of Jambudvipa but at others the two are treated as identical.[21]

In ancient times foreigners also used names to describe the part of the Indian subcontinent they came in contact with. The Iranians, for example, used for long the name of the Sindhu River, which they called 'Hindu' for the country along and beyond that river. From this the Greeks derived the Indos, which became India. In post-Hellenic Iran territorial names were given the suffix *stan* so that Hindu would become Hindustan[22] in Persian. Hsüan Tsang, the Chinese pilgrim who came to India in the early seventh century, tells us that India was called Intu but he also states that 'the names of India are various and perplexing ... people of In-tu call their country by different names'.[23] Another Chinese pilgrim, Yijing (seventh century), tells us that India is called Jambudvipa in Buddhist literature and its portions are Aryadesha (Noble land) and Madhydesha (Middle land).[24] But Hsüan Tsang defined the boundary of India with greater clarity than is seen in the previous travellers' accounts. He says that 'on three sides it is bordered by the great sea; on the north it is backed by the Snowy Mountains'.[25] Another foreigner, Alberuni, who came to India with Mahmud Ghazni (eleventh century) and is known for his encyclopaedic knowledge, also 'seems to have equated Hind (India) with the territorial spread of Bharatavarsha, extending from the mountains in the north (Himavanta) up to the sea coast in the south ... he treats the entire country as ... carrying within its folds a variety of faiths, languages and social formations'.[26] His may be treated as a fairly accurate description of the boundaries of Hindustan/India as we know it today.

It is, however, striking that India is not portrayed as a mother anywhere in our sources. The female personification of India as Bharatmata took place in the late nineteenth century and is found in the song of Dwijendralal Roy (1863-1913).[27] Its genealogy has been traced to *Unabimsa*

Purana ('The Nineteenth Purana'), a satirical play by Bhudeb Mukhopadhyay, first published anonymously in 1866. Bharatmata is identified in this text as Adhi-Bharati, the widow of Arya Swami, the embodiment of all that is essentially 'Aryan'. In the play he is killed by Yavanik, the Muslim invaders and after his sons avenge his death the kingdom of Aryapur is occupied by the British St George who tries – but fails – to persuade her to marry him.[28] Few years later Kiran Chandra Bandyopadyaya's play *Bharatmata* was published which was first staged in 1873 in the Hindu Mela patronized by the Tagores, but here the frail and widow mother is shown as asking her 'orphaned Indian children' to appeal to the 'kind Empress' and 'Mother' Victoria 'who can cure us of our particular disease'.[29] In both these works Bharatmata voices a concern for 'the impoverishment of the sons of the soil at the hands of the colonizers'.[30] The landmark in the history of Bharatmata, however, was the publication of Bankim Chandra Chattopadhyay's novel *Anandamath* in 1882.[31] It presents an evolutionary view of Bharatmata, i.e. the mother as she was in the glorious past, as she is in the miserable present (Kali) and as she will be in the bright future (Durga). The deification of the motherland and the inclusion of song *Vande Mataram* in the novel may imply that the Indian nationalism had a communal dimension right from its nascent phase. This is evident also from the first anthropomorphic portrayal of Bharatmata in 1905 as a saffron clad Vaishnava nun in a painting by Abanindranath Tagore as well as from her first cartographic representation in the Bharatmata temple built at Banaras with an 'overwhelming use of upper caste

Hindu symbols'.[32] The temple at Banaras was built by one Shyama Sharan Gupt, a lover of 'Hindutva, Hindi and Bharatmata', and was inaugurated in 1936 by Mahatma Gandhi, who lived and died for communal harmony. In independent India, an eight-storey Bharatmata temple was built by the rabidly communalist organization Vishwa Hindu Parishad (VHP) at the pilgrimage town of Haridwar and was inaugurated by the late prime minister Indira Gandhi who had, less than a decade earlier, amended the Constitution to make India a '*secular*' republic.[33] As recently as 2015 a Bharatmata temple was inaugurated at Calcutta (Kolkata) by Kesri Nath Tripathi, Governor of West Bengal and a prominent BJP leader.

Scholars have debated the history of Bharatmata for many years and have produced an impressive corpus of literature. Notwithstanding their rigorous analysis, and often hairsplitting arguments, the fact remains that through her travail of little more than a hundred years she has been wooed, claimed and reclaimed by both secular and communal forces. That is why they all joined hands to suspend a legislator who refused to chant Bharatmata ki Jai in the Maharashtra Assembly in March 2016, even though the slogan itself has become a battle cry of the champions of a Hindu theocratic state.

NOTES

1. *Rigveda* (hereafter *RV*), VIII, 24, 27. This is the only Rigvedic passage where the word *saptasindhava* is used in the sense of territory; at all other places in the *Rigveda* it is used to mean the seven rivers (*Vedic Index*, II, p. 324).

2. D.C. Sircar, *Select Inscriptions Bearing on Indian History and Civilization*, Calcutta, 1965, I, no. 91, l. 10.
3. *Amarakosha*, II.6, 8. Krishnaji Govind Oka, ed., *The Namalinganushasana: Amarakosha of Amarasimha* (with the commentary of Kshirasvamin), Delhi, 1981, p. 47.
4. According to the *Kaushitaki Upanishad* (II.13), Aryavarta was bounded on the west by Adarsana near Kurukshetra and on the east by Kalakavana near Allahabad.
5. *Kadambari*, ed. & tr. M.R. Kale, Delhi, 1968, p. 290; V.S. Agrawal, *Kadambari: Ek Sanskritik Adhyayan*, Varanasi, 1958, p. 188.
6. *Kadambari*, p. 311; Agrawal, op. cit., 1958, p. 205.
7. S.M. Ali, *The Geography of the Puranas*, Delhi, 1966, p. 109.
8. Ibid.
9. For references, see Israt Alam, 'Names for India in Ancient Indian Texts and Inscriptions', in Irfan Habib, ed., *India: Studies in the History of an Idea*, Delhi, 2005, p. 43.
10. *EI*, XIV, no. 3, ll. 5-6.
11. IV.12. *Abhidhanachintamani*, edited with an introduction by Nemichandra Shastri, with the Hindi commentary *Maniprabha* by Haragovind Sastri, Varanasi, 1964, p. 235.
12. G.P. Malalasekera, *Dictionary of Pali Proper Names*, II, pp. 941-2, sv. Jambudipa.
13. Ibid., p. 941.
14. Ibid., p. 942.
15. *Mahavamsa*, V.13; *Chulavamsa*, XXXVII.216, 246; Malalasekera, op. cit., p. 942.
16. Sircar, op. cit., no. 2, line 2.
17. Ibid., no. 56, line 9.
18. D.C. Sircar, *Studies in the Geography of Ancient and Medieval India*, Delhi, 1960, pp. 8-9.
19. Pravin Chandra Jain and Darbarilal Kothia, eds., *Jaina Purana Kosha* (in Hindi), Jain Vidya Sansthan, Srimahavirji, Rajasthan, 1993, pp. 256, 259. *Harivamsha Purana*, 5.2-13.
20. Jain and Kothia, op. cit., p. 9, n. 1.
21. Sircar, op. cit., 1960, pp. 6, 8.
22. Irfan Habib, 'India: Country and Nation – An Introductory Essay', in Irfan Habib, ed., *India – Studies in the History of an Idea*, Delhi, 2005, pp. 4-5.

23. Samuel Beal, *Si-Yu-Ki: Buddhist Records of the Western World*, London, 1884, vol. 1, p. 69.
24. *A Record of the Buddhist Religons as Practised in India and the Malay Archipelago by I-Tsing*, tr. J. Takakusu, Oxford, 1896, p. 118.
25. Beal, op. cit., p. 70.
26. Iqtidar Alam Khan, 'Concept of India in Alberuni', in Irfan Habib, ed., *India: Studies in the History of an Idea*, pp. 115-16.
27. Sugata Bose, *The Nation as Mother and Other Visions of Nationhood*, Gurgaon, 2017, p. 4.
28. Indira Chowdhury Sengupta, 'Mother India and Mother Victoria: Motherhood and Nationalism in Nineteenth Century Bengal', *South Asia Reserch*, vol. 12, no. 1, May 1993, p. 27. Sadan Jha has also drawn attention to another female figuration of the nation as Lady Hind in the cartoon magazine *Hindi Punch* published from Bombay under the editorship of Barjorjee Nowrojee in the last decade of the nineteenth century. In one of the cartoons Lady Hind and Britannica are shown as holding one flag, the flag of the empire. This is reminiscent of Bharatmata's association with Queen Victoria: see Sadan Jha, *Reverence, Resistance and Politics of Seeing the Indian National Flag*, Delhi, 2016, p. 68.
29. Chowdhury Sengupta, 'Mother India and Mother Victoria', op. cit., p. 29.
30. Indira Chowdhury, *The Frail Hero and Virile History: Gender and the Politics of Culture in Colonial Bengal* (SOAS Studies on South Asia), Delhi, 1998, p. 100.
31. Sadan Jha, 'Life and Times of Bharat Mata', *Manushi*, Issue 142; idem, *Reverence, Resistance and Politics of Seeing the Indian National Flag*, pp. 66-7.
32. Charu Gupta, 'The Icon of Mother in Late Colonial North India', *Economic and Political Weekly*, vol. 36, no. 45 (10-16 November 2001), p. 4292.
33. For details see Lise McKeen, 'Bharat Mata: Mother India and Her Militant Matriots', in John Stratton Hawley and Donna Maria Wulf, eds., *Devi: Goddesses of India*, Berkeley, 1996, pp. 250-80.

FOUR

Brahminical Intolerance in Early India*

THE CONSTRUCT OF tolerant Hinduism seems to have been of a relatively recent origin and seems to have first acquired visibility in the Western writings on India. In the seventeenth century, Francois Bernier (1620-88), the French doctor who travelled widely in India, was one of the early Europeans to speak of Hindus as a tolerant people. In the eighteenth century the German philosopher Johann Gottfried von Herder (1744-1803), the forerunner of the Romantic glorification of India, referred to the Hindus as 'mild' and 'tolerant' and as 'the gentlest branch of humanity'; and Immanuel Kant (1724-1804) said that they 'do not hate the other religions but they believe they are also right'. Such views find a more prominent place in the writings of Orientalists like William Jones, according to whom 'the Hindus ... would readily admit the truth of

*This paper is an elaboration of some points made in my presidential address to the Indian History Congress in 2006. It is reprinted here from the *Social Scientist*, nos. 516-17, May-June 2016.

the Gospel but they contend that it is perfectly consistent with their Sastras'.

It was in the nineteenth century that some Indians also began to speak of tolerance of Hindus but they clearly privileged Hinduism over other religions. Dayananda Saraswati (1824-83), who founded the Arya Samaj in 1875, claimed to believe 'in a religion based on universal values ... above the hostility of all creeds ...' but as a champion of the Vedic religion, he sharply opposed all other religions: to him Prophet Muhammad was an 'impostor' and Jesus 'a very ordinary ignorant man, neither learned nor a yogi'.[1] His contemporary Ramakrishna (1836-86) spoke of the equality of religions but in his view 'the Hindu religion alone is the Sanatana Dharma.'[2] Ramakrishna's disciple, Vivekananda (1863-1904) also laid emphasis on toleration and picked up the famous Rigvedic passage *ekamsad vipra vahudha vadanti* [The wise speak of what is One in many ways] in support of his vision that 'India alone [was] to be ... the land of toleration'. But this was incompatible with his view that ' from Pacific to the Atlantic for five hundred years blood ran all over the world' and 'that is Mohammadanism',[3] even though his Rigvedic quote has become a cliché through its endless political milking by politicians. Similar views continued to be held by some leaders in the early twentieth century. Bal Gangadhar Tilak (1856-1920), for example, couched his views in the vocabulary of tolerance and quite often cited the above Rigvedic passage but, in reality, espoused militant Hinduism. Even the Muslim hater M.S. Golwalkar (1906-73), spoke of the Hindus as the most tolerant people of the world, though this sounded like devil quoting scriptures; for, he identified Muslims, Christians and Communists as internal threats to the country.[4] It would appear that these leaders, from Dayananda to Golwalkar, used tolerance as a camouflage for Hindu belligerence, privileged Hinduism over other religions and did not provide enough space to them. Unlike them Mahatma Gandhi, who lived and died for communal harmony, genuinely found Hinduism to be the most tolerant of all religions even if his excessive pride in its inclusivism may have tended to make it exclusive.

The perception of Hinduism as a tolerant religion has predictably elicited conflicting responses from the scholarly community. On the one hand are scholars like the late Nirad C. Chaudhuri, who almost ruled out the idea of religious tolerance and asserted that 'if the familiar words about the tolerance and capacity for synthesis were true, one would be hard put to it to explain why there are such deep suspicions and enmities among the human groups in India....'[5] On the other hand, there are scholars, like Amartya Sen,[6] who have glorified religious tolerance and inclusiveness in early India.

Scholars have cited several instances to illustrate the process of mutual accommodation among the various Indian religious sects. It is held, for example, that the Buddha, the founder of a heretic religion, emerged as an *avatara* of Vishnu around the middle of the sixth century AD[7] and figured as such in several Puranas and other texts including the *Dashavataracarita* of Kshemendra (eleventh century) and *Gitagovinda* of Jayadeva[8] (twelfth century) as well as inscriptions[9]. Even Alberuni (eleventh century) refers to the Buddha *avatara* of Vishnu.[10] But, interestingly, the Buddha was also reviled as a thief and atheist[11] and Shiva is believed to have appeared on earth in the form of Shankara to combat the Buddha *avatara*, even though Shankara himself is described as an illegitimate child in a fourteenth century Vaishnava text.[12] Further, Adinatha (Risabha), the first *tirthankara* of Jainism, was accepted as an incarnation of Vishnu in the *Bhagavatapurana*,[13] and Christ was sometimes included in the incarnations of Vishnu.[14] Similarly the Muslim sect of Imam Shahis believed that the Imam was himself the tenth *avatara* of Vishnu and that the Koran was a part of the *Atharvaveda*.[15] Akbar was some times thought of as the tenth *avatara* of Vishnu[16] and Queen Victoria was accepted as a Hindu goddess when a plague broke out in Mumbai following an insult to her statue by some miscreants.[17] It is, however, missed in all this, that neither the Imam, nor Christ, nor Akbar and nor Victoria occupied an important place in the brahminical scheme of things. An oft repeated example of giving space to opposing points of view is that of Madhava Acharya (fourteenth century), who begins his *Sarvadarshanasamgraha* (Collection of All Systems), by first presenting the school of Charvakas, and then criticizes it. But it should be realized that this was in keeping with the traditional Indian practice of presenting the opponent's view (*purvapaksha*) before refuting it.

Even if we accept these instances as indicating that Brahminism gave space to other sects, there is considerable historical evidence to question the stereotype of India as a land of religious tolerance. Not only did the different brahminical sects fight among themselves of which we have plenty of evidence,[18] they also bore huge animosity towards the two heterodox religions, Buddhism and Jainism, in early India. An early evidence of this comes from the Jain canonical text, the *Acharangasuttam*, according to which monks hid themselves in the day and travelled by night lest they be suspected of being spies.[19] Similarly, the *Arthashastra* of Kautilya contemptuously describes the followers of non-Vedic sects as *vrishala* or *pashanda* (e.g. Shakyas, Ajivikas), assigns them residence at the end of or near the cremation ground and prescribes a heavy fine for inviting them to dinners in honour of the gods and the Manes.[20] By the post-Mauryan period the brahminical intolerance of the Shramanic religions seems to have struck deeper roots so that the *Mahabhashya* of Patanjali states that 'Shramanas and Brahmanas are eternal enemies' (*virodhah shashvatikah*) like the snake and mongoose[21] and the Buddhist work *Divyavadana* (third century) describes Pushyamitra Shunga as a great persecutor of Buddhists who announced a prize of one hundred *dinar* for every head of a Shramana.[22]

Brahaminical animosity towards the Shramanic religions became intense over time, especially in the early medieval period, and found its way in the philosophical discourses of the time. Uddyotakara (seventh century) is said to have refuted the arguments of the Buddhist logicians Nagarjuna and Dignag, and his views were later reinforced by Vachaspati Mishra (ninth century). Udayana, the founder of the Navya Nyaya school, also launched a sharp attack on the atheistic thesis of Buddhism in his *Atmatattvaviveka*. Outside the school of Nyaya, brahminical thinkers like Kumarila Bhatta and Shankara attacked Buddhism and Jainism; according to the latter the Buddha indulged in 'incoherent prattling ... deliberately and hatefully leading mankind into confusion...'.[23] Similarly, Madhusudana Sarasvati, the sixteenth-century Bengali commentator on the *Bhagvadgita*, held that the teachings of materialists, Buddhists and others are like those of the *mlecchas*.[24] The attitude of the orthodox philosophers found an echo in the Puranas like the *Saurapurana* [25] as well as the literary texts like the *Mattavilasa Prahasana* of Mahendravarman (seventh century) and the *Prabodhachandrodaya* of Krishna Mishra (tenth-eleventh century) which provide vulgar portrayals of the Buddhists and the Jains.[26]

The invectives against Buddhists and Jains often found expression in violence, especially from around the middle of the first millennium. According to Hsüan Tsang (seventh century) the Gauda king Shashanka, a contemporary of Harshavardhana, cut down the Bodhi tree at Gaya and removed the statue of the Buddha from the local temple, and the Huna ruler Mihirakula, a devotee of Shiva, destroyed 1,600 Buddhist *stupas* and monasteries and killed thousands of Buddhist monks and laity.[27] Kalhana (eleventh century) refers to the destruction of a Buddhist monastery by the Shaivite king Jalauka, who ruled over Kashmir after the death of his father Ashoka.[28] An important evidence of the persecution of Buddhists in Kashmir, however, dates from the reign of the king

Kshemagupta (950-8), who destroyed the Buddhist monastery Jayendravihara at Shrinagara and used the materials from it in constructing a temple called Kshemagaurishvara.[29] A Tibetan tradition has it that the Kalachuri king Karna (eleventh century) destroyed many Buddhist temples and monasteries in Magadha; and Taranatha (seventeenth century) refers to the destruction of eighty four temples in the region including Nalanda.[30] The situation in southern India seems to have been no different. A thirteenth century Alvar text, for example, tells us that the Vaishnava poet-saint Tirumankai stole a large gold image of the Buddha from a *stupa* at Nagapattinam and had it melted down for re-use in the temple which he was commissioned by the god Vishnu himself to build.[31]

While the brahminical hostility towards Buddhists has been adequately documented by scholars in recent years,[32] there is also substantial evidence of antipathy towards and persecution of Jains, especially from south India, where proponents of devotional Shaivism (Nayanars) and Vaishnavism (Alvars) consistently portrayed them as the hated 'others'. The two Shaiva saints, Appar (seventh century) and Sambandar (seventh century), denigrated the Jains in abusive language [33] and the twelfth-century hagiographical work, *Periyapuranam,* relates the legendary account of how the latter defeated the Jains in all contests and succeeded in converting the Pandyan king of Madura from Jainism to Shaivism, leading eventually to the impalement of eight thousand Jain monks. The authenticity of the impalement story is questionable,[34] but the Shaiva intolerance of Jains is corroborated by several legends found in the *Sthalapurana* of Madura[35] as well as the actual instances of brahminical violence against the Jains. Thus the conversion of the earliest known Jain cave temple in Tirunelveli district (Tamil Nadu) into a Shaiva shrine in the seventh century[36] and the depiction of scenes of violence on the walls of the Kailashnath temple of Kanchipuram[37] and on the *mandapam* of the Golden Lily tank of the Minaksi temple at Madura bear testimony to the persecution suffered by Jains in Tamil Nadu.

Evidence of the persecution of Jains also comes from other parts of India, especially Karnataka where they were a perpetual *bête noire* of the militant Shaivite Lingayat/Virashaiva sect, which started in the twelfth century. The hagiographies of its leader Basava furnish evidence of the slaughter of Jains,[38] and of the appropriation of their temples at many places by his followers like Devara Dasimayya[39] and Ekantada Ramayya[40] who are said to have destroyed 700 and 800 *basadis* respectively. According to one estimate about half of the total number of *basadis* were destroyed, and anything between 1,800 and 2,000 out of 8,000 temples were ruined.[41] The victimization of the Jains became so severe that they had to seek the intervention of the Vijayanagara ruling family; but the Virashaivas continued to persecute them, as is clear from several sixteenth-century inscriptions from the Srisailam area of Andhra Pradesh.[42] There is thus copious evidence of the Jains remaining a hated lot in medieval south India.

But all this does not mean that the adherents of Buddhism and Jainism did not retaliate. They did in fact, denounce the brahminical beliefs and practices. The Jain logician Akalanka (eighth century) and the famous scholar Hemachandra (twelfth century) were full of scorn for the Vedic practice of animal sacrifice; the latter dubbed Manu's verses supporting ritual violence as *himsashastra*.[43] The Jain contempt for the brahminical gods is evident from the statement of the seventh century commentator Jinadasa who described Maheshvara (Shiva) as 'the son of a nun who had been magically impregnated by a wizard seeking a suitable repository for his powers'[44] and from the negative portrayal of Vishnu and Krishna in the sixteenth century *Pandavapuranas*, which are the Jainized version of the *Mahabharata*.[45]

Like the Jains, the Buddhists were also hostile to Brahminism. The Buddha himself described the three Vedas as 'foolish talk' and 'a waterless desert', and their wisdom as 'a pathless jungle' and 'a perdition'.[46] In course of time the contempt of the Buddhists for brahminical religious practices seems to have become pronounced when they criticized the brahminical practice of bathing at *tirthas* and in the Ganga, and described the brahmins disparagingly as *tirthikas*. They displayed a disdainful attitude toward brahminical deities and treated them as menials and subordinate to Buddhist gods and goddesses,[47] and often portrayed them in some early medieval sculptures as being trampled upon by Buddhist gods.[48] Dharmasvamin, the Tibetan scholar who visited Bihar in the thirteenth century, tells us that the Buddhists had put an image of Shiva in front of Buddha's image so as to protect it from the wrath of non-Buddhists.[49]

Although there is evidence that the adherents of the Shramainc religions retaliated against Brahminism, it remains certain that the brahminical sects did not, as they are said to have done, practise tolerance towards non-brahminical faiths; on the contrary, they seem to have played a leading role in fomenting religious conflicts and perpetrating sectarian violence during the early medieval period and later. It is therefore not surprising that in the eleventh century Alberuni tells us that the Hindus are 'haughty, foolishly vain and self conceited' and 'believe that there is no religion like theirs'.[50]

Several factors like the conflict over the capture of temple wealth, and the competition for the material patronage of the ruling class, etc., possibly led to the animosity of the brahmins towards the Shramanas and need to be studied in detail. But there is little doubt that their belligerence owed not the least to their own martialization of which evidence is available from the Sanskrit texts which refer to the arms bearing brahmins and ascetics.[51] That they received formal training in martial arts is clear from the Jain Prakrit text *Kuvalayamala* of Udyotanasuri (eighth century), which describes a *math* at Vijaya, where students from different parts of India received instruction in such diverse subjects as archery, manoeuvring with a shield, use of the sword and the bow, fighting with a spear, fighting with clubs and free hand combat.[52] Their association with martial activities is also borne out by the *manipravala* texts especially the *Chandrotsavam* (fifteenth century) and the *Keralolapatti* (seventeenth century).[53] Literary references receive corroboration from inscriptions which clearly indicate that the brahmin students who studied Vedic lore at the religious establishments were also required to receive military training. Epigraphic references testify to the imparting of military training in temple-supported establishments, especially in Kerala, where the Kantalurshalai became famous for its role in the Chola-Chera conflict.[54] There is thus little doubt that the militarization of brahminical sects[55] and the growth of temple militias created conditions for violent conflicts between arms-bearing brahmins and the votaries of non-brahminical sects. All this makes it difficult to swallow the claim that 'Hinduism' has 'a propensity to assimilate rather than to exclude' or that tolerance is the very essence of 'Hinduism qua Hinduism'.[56]

NOTES

1. For an outright denunciation of Islam and Christianity by Dayananda see his *Satyarth Prakash*, Delhi, rpt. 1977, chapters XIII and XIV.
2. *The Gospel of Sri Ramakrishna (Sri Sri Kathamrita),* tr. Swami Nikhilanand, New York, 2007, p. 642 cited in Jyotirmaya Sharma, *Cosmic Love and Human Apathy: Swami Vivekananda's Restatement of Religion,* Delhi, 2013, p. 91.uH
3. Lecture delivered at the Shakespeare club of Pasadena, California, USA, on 3 February 1900. See *The Complete Works of Swami Vivekananda*, Mayavati Memorial Edition, Calcutta, vol. 4, 1978, p. 126.
4. M.S. Golwalkar, *Bunch of Thoughts,* Bangalore, rpt., 1996, chapter XVI, pp. 177-201.
5. Nirad C. Chaudhuri, *The Continent of Circe*, London, 1965, p. 39.
6. *The Argumentative Indian*, London, 2005, pp. 3-33.
7. R.C. Hazra, *Studies in the Puranic Records on the Hindu Rites and Customs*, Delhi, 1975, pp. 41-2; Wendy Doniger O'Flaherty, *The Origin of Evil in Hindu Mythology,* Delhi, 1988, pp. 204-11.

8. Hazra, op. cit., p. 41.
9. H. Krishna Sastri, *Memoirs of the Archaeological Survey of India*, vol. 26, rpt., Delhi, 1991, pp. 5ff.
10. Edward Sachau, *Alberuni's India*, London, 1910, p. 380.
11. *Ramayana*, II.109.34 cited in P.V. Kane, *History of Dharmashastra*, vol. II, pt. 2, Poona, 1974, p. 721.
12. O'Flaherty, op. cit., pp. 208-9; Phyllis Granoff, 'Holy Warriors: A Preliminary Study of Some Biographies of Saints and Kings in Classical Indian Tradition', *Journal of Indian Philosophy*, vol. 12 (1984), p. 296.
13. Padmanabh S. Jaini, *Collected Papers on Jaina Studies*, Delhi, 2000, pp. 343-4; Ravi M. Gupta and Kenneth R. Valpey, *The Bhagavata Purana*, 2013, pp. 157-9.
14. A. Danielou, *Hindu Polytheism*, New York, 1964, p. 12.
15. W. Ivanow, 'The Sect of Imam Shah in Gujrat', *Journal of the Bombay Branch of Royal Asiatic Society*, vol. 12 (1936), pp. 19-70.
16. J. Talboys Wheeler, ed., *Early Travels in India (16th and 17th Centuries)*, rpt., Delhi, 1974, p. 78; Audrey Truschke, *Culture of Encounters: Sanskrit at the Mughal Court*, Delhi, 2017, pp. 39-40.
17. E.W. Hopkins, 'The Divinity of Kings', *Journal of the American Oriental Society*, vol. 51 (1931), p. 314.
18. D.N. Jha, 'Of Conflict, Conversion and Cow', in D.N. Jha, ed., *Contesting Symbols and Stereotypes: Essays on Indian History and Culture*, Delhi, 2013, pp. 53-6.
19. *Acharangasutta*, tr. H. Jacobi, Sacred Books of the East, XXII, II.3.1.10.
20. *Arthashastra*, II.4.23; III.20.16.
21. *The Vyakarana Mahabhashya of Patanjali*, 2.4.9, 3rd edn., Poona, 1962, vol. I, p. 476.
22. *Divyavadana*, ed. E.B. Cowell and R.A. Neil, Cambridge, 1886, pp. 433-4.
23. Wilhelm Halbfass, *Tradition and Reflection: Exploration in Indian Thought*, Albany, 1991, p. 57. For Shankara's refutation of Buddhist philosophical positions see D.H.H. Ingalls, 'Samkara's Arguments Against the Buddhists', *Philosophy East and West*, vol. 3, no. 4 (January 1954), pp. 291-306.
24. Wilhelm Halbfass, *India and Europe: An Essay in Understanding*, Delhi, 1990, p. 361.

25. *Saurapurana*, 64.44; 38.54.
26. *Mattavilasa Prahasana* of Mahendravikramavarman, ed. and tr. N.P. Uni, Trivandrum, 1973, p. 49; *Prabodhachandrodaya* of Kishna Mishra, ed. and tr. Sita Nambiar, Delhi, 1998, Act III, verse 9.
27. Samuel Beal, *Si-Yu-Ki: Buddhist Records of the Western World*, Delhi, 1969, pp. 171-2.
28. *Rajatarangini* of Kalhana, I.140-4.
29. Ibid., VI.171-3.
30. Debiprasad Chattopadhyaya, ed., *Taranatha's History of Buddhism in India*, Delhi, 1970 (rpt. 1990), pp. 141-2.
31. Richard H. Davis, *Lives of Indian Images*, first Indian edition, Delhi, 1999, p. 83.
32. Johannes Bronkhorst, *Buddhism in the Shadow of Brahmanism*, Leiden, 2011; Giovanni Verardi, *Hardships and Downfall of Buddhism in India*, Delhi, 2011; Tiziana Lorenzetti, 'Political and Social Dimensions as Reflected in Medieval Indian Sculpture', Proceedings of International Conference *In the Shadow of the Golden Age: Art and Identity in South Asia from Gandhara to the Modern Age*, Bonn, 2011.
33. Indira Viswanathan Peterson, 'Sramanas Against the Tamil Way', in John Cort, ed., *Open Boundaries: Jain Communities and Culture in Indian History,* New York, 1998, p. 171.
34. For an insightful discussion of the impalement legend, see Paul Dundas, *The Jains,* London, 1992, pp. 109-10; Richard H. Davis, 'The Story of the Disappearing Jains', in John Cort, op. cit., pp. 213-14.
35. P.B. Desai, *Jainism in South India and Some Jaina Epigraphs*, Sholapur, 1957, p. 82.
36. Romila Thapar, *Cultural Transaction and Early India*, Delhi, 1987, p. 17; K.R. Srinivasan, 'South India', in A. Ghosh, ed., *Jaina Art and Architecture*, vol. 2, Delhi, 1975; John Cort, op. cit., pp. 107-8.
37. R.N. Nandi, *Social Roots of Religion in Ancient India*, Calcutta, 1986, p. 97.
38. Velcheru Narayana Rao, *Siva's Warriors: The Basava Purana of Palkuriki Somanatha*, Princeton, 1990, pp. 200-13.
39. Shantinath Dibbad, 'The Construction, Destruction and Renovation of Jaina Basadis: A Historical Perspective', in Julia

B. Hegewald, ed., *The Jain Heritage: Distinction, Decline and Resilience*, Delhi, 2011, p. 71.

40. Ibid., pp. 69-70.
41. Ibid., pp. 63-76.
42. Desai, op. cit., p. 23.
43. *Yogashastra* of Hemachandra, ed., Muni Jambuvijaya, 3 vols, Bombay, 177-86, II.33-40.
44. For similar anti-brahminical statements in Jain literature see Dundas, op. cit., pp. 200-6.
45 Jaini, op. cit., p. 353.Cf. Dundas, op. cit., pp. 200-6.
46 Tevijjasutta, *Dighanikaya*, ed. Bhikhu Jagdish Kassapa, Nalanda-Devanagari-Pali Series, Patna, 1958.
47. *Sadhanamala*, XLI.II, nos. 260, 263-4, etc., cited in B.N. Sharma, 'Religious Tolerance and Intolerance as Reflected in Indian Sculptures', *Journal of the Ganganath Jha Research Institute*, Umesh Mishra Commemoration Volume, 1970, p. 665.
48. Sharma, op. cit., pp. 65-6.
49. G. Roerich, *Biography of Dharmasvamin*, Patna, 1959, p. 64.
50. Sachau, op. cit., p. 22.
51. G.S. Ghurye, *Indian Sadhus,* Bombay, 1964, chapter VI.
52. *Kuvalayamala* of Udyotansuri, pt. I, ed. A.N. Upadhye, Bombay, 1959, pp. 150-1. Also see Shanta Rani Sharma, *Society and Culture in Rajasthan AD 700-900*, Delhi, 1996, p. 231.
53. Kesavan Veluthat, *Brahmana Settlements in Kerala*, Calicut, 1978, Appendix II, pp. 102-15.
54. Ibid.; M.G.S. Narayanan, 'Kantalur Shalai: New Light on the Nature of Aryan Expansion to South India', *Proceedings of the Indian History Congress*, Jabalpur, 1970, pp. 125-36.
55. Ghurye, op. cit., chapter VI.
56. Arvind Sharma, 'Some Misunderstandings of the Hindu Approach to Religious Plurality', *Religion*, vol. 8 (Autumn 1978), p. 145.

FIVE

Whatever Happened to Buddhist Monuments

THE HINDUTVA IDEOLOGUES look at the ancient period of Indian history as a golden age marked by social harmony devoid of any religious violence and portray the middle ages as a phase of a reign of terror unleashed by the Muslim rulers on Hindus. Central to their perception is their belief that the Muslim rulers indiscriminately demolished Hindu temples and broke Hindu idols; they relentlessly propagate the canard that 60,000 Hindu temples were demolished during the Muslim rule, though there is hardly any credible evidence for the destruction of more than eighty. On the other hand even a cursory survey of historical evidence shows that demolition and desecration of rival religious establishments and appropriation of their idols was not uncommon in India before the advent of Islam.

I

There existed many brahminical and non-brahminical religions and their sects in ancient India. Their adherents were not always friendly and mutually accommodative but were, in fact, very often hostile to one another. The two brahminical sects, Vaishnavism and Shaivism, fought among themselves, and they both were constantly at loggerheads with the followers of the Shramanic religions (Buddhism and Jainism). In the present paper I propose to present a limited survey of the desecration, destruction and appropriation of the Buddhist *stupas*, monasteries and other structures by the brahminical forces, evidence for which begins to be available towards the end of the rein of Ashoka, who is credited with making Buddhism a world religion. A tradition recorded in the eleventh century Kashmiri text, *Rajatarangini* of Kalhana, mentions one of his sons, Jalauka. Unlike his father he was a Shaivite, and destroyed Buddhst monasteries.[1] If this is given credence, the attacks on Shramanic religions seem to have begun either in the lifetime of Ashoka or soon after his death. Another early evidence of the persecution of Sharamanas comes for the post-Mauryan period recorded in the third century Buddhist Sanskrit work, *Divyavadana*, which describes the brahmin ruler Pushyamitra Shunga (185-149 BC) as a great persecutor of Buddhists: he is said to have marched out with a large army, destroying *stupas*, burning monasteries and killing monks as far as Sakala (Sialkot), where he announced a prize of one hundred *dinar* for every head of a Shramana.[2] Added to this is the evidence from the grammarian Patanjali (150 BC), a contemporary of the Shungas, who famously stated in his *Mahabhashya* (2.4.9) that the brahmins and Shramanas are eternal enemies like the snake and the mongoose. All this taken together means that the stage was set for brahminical onslaught on Buddhism during the post-Mauryan period especially under Pushyamitra Shunga who may have destroyed the Ashokan Pillared Hall and Kukutarama monastery at Pataliputra (modern Patna) in his bid to obliterate an important symbol of Mauryan power.[3]

The possibility of the Shunga assault on Buddhist monuments is supported by the layers of debris and the evidence of desertion of sites found at many centres of Buddhism, notably in Madhya Pradesh. For example Sanchi in Raisen district, which was an important Buddhist site since the time of Ashoka, has yielded evidence of vandalization of several edifices during the Shunga period;[4] similar evidence comes from the nearby places like Satdhara (Katni district) and Deurkothar (Rewa district).[5] The destruction and appropriation of Buddhist sites continued in Madhya Pradesh even after the Shunga rule. At Ahmedpur, for instance, a brahminical temple seems to have been constructed on a *stupa* base in the fifth century[6] and icons have been found at several sites around Vidisha which were transformed into Shaivite or Jaina places of worship around the eighth century.[7] More than 250 km in the north-east of Vidisha a Buddhist establishment existed at Khajuraho before it emerged as a major temple town from the tenth century onwards under the Chandellas.[8] Here the Ghantai temple appears to have been built on the remains of a Buddhist monument in the ninth or tenth century[9] by the Jains who also may have had a strong presence in the region.[10]

Outside Madhya Pradesh, there are many sites where destruction and appropriation of Buddhist sites and monuments seem to have taken place in the post-Mauryan centuries. For example, at Mathura, a flourishing town in western Uttar Pradesh during the Kushana period, some of the present day brahminical temples like those of Bhuteshwar and Gokarneshwar were originally Buddhist sites in ancient period.[11] Here the Katra Mound, a Buddhist centre during Kushana times, became a Hindu religious site in the early medieval period.[12] More than 500 km from here in the south-east, at Kaushambi, near Allahabad, the destruction and burning of the great Ghositaram monastery has been attributed to the Shungas more specifically to Pushyamitra.[13] Less than 150 km east, Sarnath, near Varanasi, where the Buddha had delivered his first sermon, became the target of brahminical assault. This was followed by the construction of brahminical buildings like Court 36 and Structure 136,[14] probably in the Gupta period by re-using Mauryan materials in front of the so-called Main Shrine;[15] this shrine itself was built above the ruins of a large destroyed Ashokan *stupa*. Towards the end of the Gupta period the site was occupied by the Buddhists to be reoccupied by non-Buddhists again.[16]

Other towns associated with the Buddha were also either vandalized or appropriated. The Chinese pilgrim Fa-hsien, who visited India during the Gupta period (399-414), presents a rather dismal picture of Sravasti, where the Buddha spent much of his life. Here the brahmins seem to have appropriated a Kushana Buddhist site where a temple with *Ramayana* panels was constructed during the Gupta period.[17] In fact the general scenario of Buddhist establishments in Uttar Pradesh was so bad that in the Sultanpur district alone no less than forty-nine Buddhist sites seem to have been destroyed by fire 'when Brahminism won its final victories over Buddhism'.[18] In north Bihar, Vaishali was an important city associated with the Buddha where he had spent a few years before proceeding to Kushinagar. Fa-hsien does not seem to have spent much time there and merely mentions the existence of a *stupa* erected by the courtesan Amradarika. But another contemporary Chinese account, Waiguo shi of Zhi Sengzai (265-420) describing the situation prior to his visit reports that the house of Vimalkirti at Vaishali was destroyed.[19]

In the post-Gupta centuries several brahminical thinkers and philosophers of different schools of thought from various parts of the country launched a massive ideological onslaught on Buddhists which coincided with sustained attack on their establishments. The Chinese Buddhist pilgrim and traveller Hsüan Tsang, who visited India from 631 to 645 during the reign of Harshavardhana, states that the Huna ruler Mihirakula (502-30 CE), a devotee of Shiva, destroyed 1,600 Buddhist *stupas* and monasteries and killed thousands of Buddhist monks and laity.[20] He further tells us that 1,000 *sangharamas* in Gandhara were 'deserted' and were in 'ruins'[21] and describes 1,400 *sangharamas* in Uddiyana as 'generally waste and desolate'.[22] Although he does not specifically attribute the desertion and destruction of these monuments to any particular individual, much of this destruction was wrought possibly by Mihirakula whom the Chinese sources describe 'as the incarnation of a devil intent on destroying the True Dharma'[23] and the *Rajatarangini* of Kalhana (twelfth century) refers to as 'a man of violent acts and resembling Kala (Death)'.[24]

In some parts of the country, as in Kashmir, the rulers ordered the demolition of temples and Buddhist establishments both as a personal vendetta as well as a matter of policy. Kalhana makes an interesting reference to king Nara who, angered by the Buddhist monk who seduced his wife, 'burned thousands of viharas'[25] in revenge. He also speaks of the tenth century king Kshemagupta (AD 950-8), who destroyed the Buddhist monastery Jayendravihara at Shrinagara and used its materials for the construction of the Kshemagaurishvara temple.[26] Among the Kashmir kings mentioned in the text, Harshadeva (AD 1089-1111) was the most notorious. He systematically plundered and demolished Hindu and Buddhist temples for wealth and appointed one Udayaraja as *devotpatanna-nayaka*, the special officer to supervise the destruction of temples and uprooting of idols.[27]

Sources provide evidence of the brahminical vandalism of Buddhist monuments also in the eastern region of the Indian subcontinent. Hsüan Tsang tells us that the king Shashanka of Gauda, a contemporary of Harsha, cut down the Bodhi tree at Bodh Gaya in Bihar, the place of the Buddha's enlightenment, removed the statue of the Buddha from the local temple, and ordered it to be replaced by the image of Maheshvara; according to one view,[28] however, the Shaivites had already appropriated the site and Shashanka merely restored Shiva's worship. Although Bodh Gaya came under the Buddhist control again during the period of the Pala rulers who were Buddhists, the place has, in fact, remained a site of religious contestation throughout Indian history; for traditional accounts and archaeological evidence suggest that the Mahabodhi temple was repeatedly destroyed and rebuilt. At the nearby Gaya, which figures prominently as a *pitritirtha* (where ancestral rites could be performed), in early medieval Puranic texts, a site was appropriated in the mid-eleventh century to establish a Vishnu temple, with its floor and railing made of re-used material.[29] The modern Vishnupada temple was, however, built by the queen Ahilya Bai Holkar of Indore in the late eighteenth century.

Less than a hundred kilometres north-east of Gaya was located the internationally reputed Buddhist university at Nalanda with a vast monastic complex where Hsüan Tsang spent more than five years. Here a brahminical temple (probably Shaivite) was constructed in the mid-seventh century (and hence soon after Hsüan Tsang's visit) behind Monasteries 7 and 8 on the eastern row of *viharas*. Unlike the Buddhist buildings, which were all built of bricks, this temple was built entirely with huge dressed stone and was completely out of place with regard to the general layout of the monasteries, and occupied what was essentially a Buddhist site.[30] Evidence reveals a 'complex history of destruction, abandonment and reoccupation' also at Monasteries 1 and 4.[31] But the ultimate destruction of the Nalanda Mahavihara was caused by the 'Hindu fanatics' who set to fire its library.[32] The popular view, however, wrongly attributes this conflageration to Bakhtiyar Khilji who never went there but, in fact, sacked the nearby Odantapuri Mahavihara at modern Bihar Sharif. Bakhtiyar is also believed to have destroyed the Vikramashila Mahavihara, the centre of Vajrayana, located at modern Antichak near Bhagalpur in Jharkhand and founded in the eighth century by the Pala ruler Dharmapala. But this too is not borne out by evidence which seems to attribute its destruction to a conflagration and the attack probably by the Sena rulers of Bengal who were inimical to Buddhism.[33] Like them the Kalachuri king Karna (eleventh century), who was also hostile to Buddhism, had earlier destroyed many Buddhist temples and monasteries in Magadha;[34] in this region, according to Taranatha (seventeenth century), eighty-four temples were destroyed including Nalanda.[35] The Senas, in fact, invaded Buddhist establishments also in Bengal. For example, at Somapura Mahavihar (Paharpur, Bangladesh), founded by Dharmapala, the presence of huge heaps of charcoal and ashes in the remains, an epigraphic reference to the fire caused by 'an approaching army' and to the death of a monk in the conflagration have been interpreted as evidence of its destruction by the orthodox forces represented by the Senas.[36]

Ancient Bengal provides several other instances of transformation or appropriation of smaller Buddhist sites by the brahminical elements. At Bankura, for example, the Siddheshwar temple was built on the *stupas*, and at

Gokulmedh (Mahasthan) and Birampur[37] (Dinajpur) Buddhist monuments were converted into brahminical temples around twelfth or thirteenth century. An instance of the brahminical appropriation of a Buddhist temple has come to light last year at Basudevpur, Bochaganj, Dinajpur in Bangladesh.[38]

South-west of Bengal, Buddhism struck roots in Orissa on the eastern coast during the reign of Ashoka (third century BC) and remained greatly influential in the region for centuries. It received a setback during the seventh century when Shashanka conquered Utkal and Kongoda (northern and southern Orissa) and the Shaivite groups of Pashupatas possibly made their first attempt to convert Bhubaneswar into a *tirtha*.[39] But Buddhist influence seems to have been much undermined after the end of the Bhaumakara rule around the middle of the tenth century. This is evident from the destruction/abandonment of Buddhist structures and the mushrooming of brahminical buildings over or near them during the rule of the Somavamshis (AD 822-1110) and the Eastern Gangas (AD 1078-1434). Even the Jagannath temple at Puri, one of the most prominent brahminical pilgrimage centres in eastern India, built in the twelfth century during the rule the Eastern Ganga ruler Anantavarman Chodaganga Deva, is said to have been constructed on a Buddhist site.[40] While the Buddhist antecedent of the Jagannath temple may be contested, there is hardly any doubt that the temples of Purneshvara, Kedareshvara, Kanteshvara, Someshvara and Angeshvara, all in the Puri district, were either built on Buddhist *viharas* or made of the material derived from them. This is true also of the Dakshineshvara temple at Bagalpur and Taila Math near Madhava (both in the Cuttack district). Similarly the Agikhia Math in Sohagpur (Puri district), and Kandhei Math near Bajapur (Khorda) and a Shaiva temple in Kopari (Balasore district) were all built on Buddhist buildings or their ruins.[41] Examples of similar brahminical appropriations are available also in the neighbouring Chattisgarh. At Sirpur or Shripur (Raipur district) the main temple and the attached monastery built by the monk Anandaprabhu during the reign of Mahashivagupta Balarjuna (AD 725-86) were appropriated by the Shaivites, who carried out extensive repairs and changes[42] and took over other monasteries in the area as well.[43]

In Maharashtra, which is home to nearly a thousand rock cut caves and temples, there may be many sites where Buddhist monuments were either destroyed or appropriated but, in the absence of a comprehensive study only three of them may be mentioned here. They are Ter or ancient Tagara in Osmanabad district, Karle near Lonavala in the Pune district and Ellora in Aurangabad district. At Ter an apsidal temple was converted into a Hindu temple of Trivikrama whose damaged stone image dates to the early Chalukyan period;[44] at Karle the votive *stupa* in the Buddhist rock-cut monastery was reconstructed into a large lingam so that the Buddhist site could become a Shaiva temple;[45] and at Ellora iconographies reveal that an 'enormous amount of violence'[46] took place there during the Rashtrakuta period and the original Buddhist caves were converted into brahminical temples.[47]

In Andhra Pradesh there are several instances of brahminical appropriation of Buddhist sites. At Chezerla (Guntur district) a Buddhist monastery was converted into Kapoteshvara temple during the early medieval period;[48] at Nagarjunakonda there seems to have taken place a 'ruthless' and 'appalling' destruction of buildings during the time of the Guptas,[49] though the local tradition attributes it to the followers of Shankaracharya.[50] At Amaravati, where Shaivite presence is attested during the eastern Chalukya period, a Shiva temple was built a few metres away from the Great Stupa on the bank of the Krishna which was possibly an encroachment on a Buddhist site.[51] Not far from here, at Dhanyakataka (modern Dharanikota), Hsüan Tsang tells us, the 'numerous' *sangharamas* were mostly deserted and ruined', possibly indicating violent changes in the region.[52] To all this may be added the Buddhist caves at Undavalli, near Vijayawada, which seems to have been appropriated by the brahminical sects.[53]

In the neighbouring state of Karnataka which had been a centre of Buddhism from the time of Ashoka, we come across two important places where Buddhist monasteries were clearly appropriated by the Shaivites. One was Aihole in north Karnataka, the cultural capital of the Chalukyas. Here the Lad Khan temple, dating to the sixth century, was originally a simple square hall and possibly served as the central hall of a Buddhist *vihara*. But it was transformed into a temple devoted to Surya-Narayana, with walls, windows, cellar and roof shrine.[54] The other example of conversion/appropriation comes from the vicinity of

Mangalore, in south Karnataka, where a Buddhist monastery and temple called Kadarika *vihara* was transformed into a Shaivite temple in 1068.[55]

The situation seems to have been somewhat confusing in the far south because Hsüan Tsang mentions Chola country as distinct from Dravida country. The former, according to him, 'is deserted and wild, ... the sangharamas are ruined and dirty'; and the latter's capital, Kachipuram, was home to 'some hundred of sangharamas and 10,000 priests'.[56] There may be some confusion duc to Hsüan Tsang's use of the 'Chola' and 'Dravida' as two distinct regions but there is hardly any doubt that in the southern region Buddhism suffered a major setback as a result of the brahminical movement led by Shankara who is believed to have set up one of his four *maths* at Kanchipuram. The discovery of several Buddha images around the Kamakshi temple leads one to believe that it was built on a Buddhist building.[57] It has been suggested that this well known temple was in all probability originally a shrine of goddess Tara associated with Buddhism and it was here that the Kamakotipitha was established.[58] Another known example of appropriation comes from Tiruppadirippuliyur (near Cuddalore) where the Gunadharishwara temple was built on the Buddhist ruins. An interesting example of the appropriation and re-use of Buddhist images is that of the Vaishnava poet-saint Tirumankai who stole a large gold image of the Buddha from a *stupa* at Nagapattinam and had it melted down for re-use in the temple which he was commissioned by the god Vishnu himself to build.[59] Appropriations may have taken place at several other centres of Buddhism in south India and need to be examined.

Our survey does not cover the entire country; nor can it claim to cover fully even the smaller areas it has touched upon. But it shows that brahminism never came to terms with Buddhism though there is much evidence of interaction and mutual borrowings between them, which has been discussed by many scholars. Contrary to the Hindutva view of the ancient period of Indian history as a golden age marked by social and religious harmony, our survey provides evidence of violent religious conflict before the advent of Islam. It shows that demolition and desecration of rival religious establishments was fairly common. Not only did the brahmins vandalize and/or appropriate Buddhist sites and monuments; they targeted the Jaina monuments as well, but that is a different story.

NOTES

1. *Rajatarangini*, I.140-4.
2. *Divyavadana*, ed. E.B. Cowell and R.A. Neil, Cambridge, 1886, pp. 433-4.
3. *Ashokavadana*: 133 (p. 293) cited in Giovanni Verardi, *Hardships and Downfall of Buddhism in India*, Delhi, 2011, p. 101.
4. Debala Mitra, *Sanchi*, Delhi, 1957, pp. 13, 35, 46; John Marshall.
5. P.K. Mishra, 'Does Newly Excavated Buddhist Temple Provide a Missing Link?', *Archaeology*, 4 April 2001. http://archive.archaeology.org/online/news/deorkothar/#
6. Verardi, op. cit., p. 182.
7. Ibid., p. 326. For a discussion of changing religious landscape in Madhya Pradesh see Anne Casile, 'Changing Religious Landscapes in Gupta Times: Archaeological Evidence from the Area of Baḍoh-Paṭhāri in Central India', *South Asian Studies*, 2014, vol. 30,

no. 2, pp. 245-68, http://dx.doi.org/10.1080/02666030.2014.962303.

8. Devangana Desai, 'The Buddha Image at Khahuraho and its significance', in D.N. Jha, ed., *The Complex Heritage of Early India: Essays in Memory of R.S. Sharma*, Delhi, 2014, pp. 671-9.
9. Ibid., p. 300. This is based on the fact that an inscribed Buddha image was found near the temple by Cunningham: Devangana Desai, *The Religious Imagery of Khajurao*, Mumbai, 1996, p. 34.
10. Verardi, op. cit., p. 300.
11. R.C. Sharma, 'Mathura: A Case Study', in Catherine Asher and Thomas Metcalf, *Perceptions of South Asia's Visual Past*, Delhi, 1994, p. 118.
12. Ibid.
13. Steven L. Danver (ed.), *Popular Controversies in World History*, vol. 2, Santa Barbara, 2011, p. 96.
14. *Archaeological Survey of India: Annual Report*, 1906-7, p. 79.
15. D.R. Sahni, *Guide to Buddhist Remains at Sarnath*, 1923, p. 22 R.
16. Verardi, op. cit., p. 421.
17. Ibid., p. 137; *Archaeological Survey of India: Annual Report*, 1907-8, pp. 81-130; also see J.H. Marshall, 'Archaeological Exploration in India, 1907-8', *The Journal of the Royal Asiatic Society of Great Britain and Ireland* (October 1908), p. 1100.
18. A. Fuhrer, *The Monumental Antiquities and Inscriptions in the North-Western Provinces and Oudh*, Varanasi, 1969, p. 325.
19. Verardi, op. cit., pp. 137-8.
20. Samuel Beal, *Si-Yu-Ki: Buddhist Records of the Western World*, Delhi, 1969, pp. 171-2.
21. Ibid., p. 98.
22. Ibid., p. 120.
23. David Wellington, 'Early Forebodings of the Death of Buddhism', *Numen*, vol. 27 (1980), p. 129.
24. *Rajatarangini*, I. 289.
25. Ibid., I.200.
26. Ibid., VI. 171-3.
27. Ibid., I.1091.
28. Verardi., op. cit., p. 407; Prudence R. Myer, 'The Great Temple

at Bodh-Gaya', *The Art Bulletin*, vol. 40, no. 4 (December 1958), pp. 277-98.

29. R.L. Mitra, *Buddha Gaya: The Hermitage of Sakya Muni*, Calcutta, 1878, rpt., Delhi, 1972, p. 125; Jacob N. Kinnard, 'When Is The Buddha Not the Buddha? The Hindu/Buddhist Battle over Bodhgayā and Its Buddha Image', *Journal of the American Academy of Religion,* vol. 66, no. 4 (Winter 1998), pp. 817-39, Debjani Paul, 'Antiquity of the Visnupada at Gaya Tradition and Archaeology', *East and West*, vol. 35, nos. 1/3, September 1985, pp. 103-43.
30. Krishna Deva and V.S. Agrawala, 'The Stone Temple at Nalanda', *Journal of UP Historical Society*, vol. 23 (1950), pp. 198-12; Krishna Deva, 'Stone Temple No. 2 at Nalanda', *Journal of Indian Society of Oriental Art*, ns, vol. 11 (1980), pp. 80-4.
31. Ibid.
32. D.N. Jha, 'Looking for a Hindu Identity', Presidential Address, Indian History Congress, Viswa Bharati, 2006, p. 39, fn. 163 http://www.sacw.net/India_History/dnj_Jan06.pdf Cf . Verardi, op. cit., p. 363.
33. R.K. Choudhary, 'Decline of the University of Vikramasila', *Journal of Indian History*, vol. LVI (ii), 1976, pp. 213-35.
34. V.V. Mirashi, *Corpus Inscriptionum Indicarum*, IV, pt. 1 (?) Inscriptions of the kings of the Kalacuri Cedi Era, pp. xci-xcii.
35. Debiprasad Chattopadhyaya, ed., *Taranatha's History of Buddhism in India*, Delhi, 1970 (rpt. 1990), pp. 141-2.
36. Swadhin Sen, 'Crossing the Boundaries of Archaeology of Somapura: Alternative Approaches and Perspectives', *Pratnatattva*, vol. 20 (June 2014), pp. 49-79. K.N. Dikshit, *Excavations at Paharpur*, MASI, no. 55, Delhi, 1938, pp. 20, 29; H. Sastri, 'Nalanda and its Epigraphic Material', *Archaeological Survey of India Memoirs*, no. 66, Delhi, 1999, p. 103; N. Dutt, *Buddhist Monasteries in India*, London, 1962, p. 376, N. Ray, *Bangaleer Itihas*, Calcutta, BS 1387, p. 419.
37. Swadhin Sen, 'Interpreting Transformation of Material Culture with Reference to Stratigraphy: Report on the Excavation at Bowalar Mandap Mound', Birampur, Dinajpur, Bangladesh.

38. An email communication (dated 18 September 2016) from Professor Swadhin Sen of Jahangirnagar University, Dhaka, Bangladesh, who has carried out the excavation at the site.
39. Verardi, op. cit., p. 282.
40. R.L. Mitra, *Antiquities of Orissa*, II, rpt., Calcutta, 1963, p. 179; cf. Verardi, op. cit., p. 375.
41. Verardi, op. cit., pp. 372-8.
42. A. Ghosh, *Encyclopedia of Indian Archaeology*, Delhi, 1989, p. 411. Verardi, op. cit., pp. 310-11.
43. *Indian Archaeology: A Review*, 1954-5, pp. 24-6; ibid., 1955-6, pp. 26-7.
44. H. Ter.-Tagara Cousens, 'Archaeological Survey of India 1902-03', pp. 195-204. Cf. M.S. Mate, 'The Trivikrama Temple at Ter', *Bulletin of the Deccan College Research Institute*, vol. 18 (January 1957), pp. 1-4.
45. Romila Thapar, 'Destroying Shrines', *Frontline*, 9 January 2015.
46. Verardi., op. cit., p. 271.
47. Krishna Kumar, 'The Buddhist Origin of Some Brahminical Cave-Temples at Ellora', *East and West*, vol. 26, no. 3/4 (September-December 1976), pp. 359ff.
48. M.R. Rao, *Select Andhra Temples*, Hyderabad, 1970, pp. 7-9.
49. Verardi, op. cit., pp. 167-8.
50. A.H. Longhurst, *Buddhist Antiquities at Nagarjunakonda*, Madras Presidency, Archaelogical Survey of India Memoirs, no. 54, Delhi, 1938, p. 6.
51. Robert Knox, *Amaravati, Buddhist Sculptures from the Great Stupa*, London, 1992, pp. 15-16.
52. Beal, op. cit., II, p. 221; cf. Verardi, op. cit., p. 176.
53. K.R. Srinivasan, 'Rock-cut Monuments', in A. Ghosh, ed., *Archaeological Remains, Monuments and Museums*, Delhi, 1964, pt. 1, pp. 138-9.
54. Aschwin Lippe, 'Additions and Replacements in Early Chālukya Temples' *Archives of Asian Art*, vol. 23 (1969/70), p. 13.
55. P.S. Jaini, *Collected Papers on Buddhist Studies*, Delhi, 2001, pp. 147-8.
56. Beal, op. cit., II, pp. 227, 229.
57. T.A. Gopinatha Rao, 'Bauddha Vestiges in Kanchipura', *Indian*

Antiquary, vol. 44 (1915), pp. 127-9; Cf. Peter Schalk (ed.), *Buddhism among Tamils in Tamilakam and lam*, part 3, Uppsala, 2013, pp. 59ff.

58. T.N. Ramachandran, *The Nagapattinam and Other Buddhist Bronzes in the Chennai Museum,* revd. edn., Chennai, 2005, p. 12.
59. Richard H. Davis, *Lives of Indian Images*, first Indian edition, Delhi, 1999, p. 83.

SIX

What the Gods Drank!*

I WAS AMUSED to read in the media that there was a ruckus in the Rajya Sabha recently over the alleged association of Hindu deities with alcohol. Since the objectionable remarks were expunged I am not able to refer specifically to the god or to the MP who mentioned him. Our politicians may not be well versed in all our ancient lore specially because knowledge of the past is not their strong point; but it is not too much to expect that they should have the basic idea of the qualities and activities of the divinities whom they worship and pigheadedly defend. For constraints of space it is not possible to discuss here the traits of all those gods and goddesses who used alcohol, but I would like to draw the attention of your readers to only few of them who binged regularly on intoxicating drinks.

In the Vedic texts Soma was the name of a god as well as of a plant from which a heady drink of that name was

*A shorter version of this paper was published in the *Indian Express* on 29 July 2017.

derived and was offered to gods in most of the sacrifices; one entire section of the *Rigveda* is devoted to the preparation of *soma*. It was different from another intoxicating drink, *sura*, which was meant for the common people. *Soma* was a favourite beverage of the Vedic deities and was offered in most of the sacrifices performed to please gods like Indra, Agni, Varun and Maruts and so on, whose names occur frequently in the *Rigveda*. Of them Indra, who is known by forty-five epithets and to whom the largest number of Rigvedic hymns – 250 out of more than a thousand – are dedicated, was the most important. A god of war and wielder of the thunderbolt, rowdy and adulterous and potbellied from excessive drinking, he is described in the Vedic passages as a prodigious imbiber and dipsomaniac; he is said to have drunk three lakes of *soma* before slaying the dragon Vritra. Like Indra, several other Vedic gods were *soma*-drinkers but they do not seem to have been habitual tipplers. Agni, for example, may have drunk moderately though a detailed analysis will show that teetotalism was unknown to the Vedic gods and drinking was an essential feature of sacrifices performed in their honour. In a ritual performed at the beginning of the Vajapeya sacrifice a round of collective drinking took place in which a sacrificer offered five cups to Indra as well as seventeen cups of *soma* and seventeen cups of *sura* to 34 gods.

Like the Vedic texts, the Epics provide evidence of the use of intoxicating drinks by those who enjoy godly status in Hindu religion. In the *Mahabharata*, for example, Sanjay describes Krishna (an incarnation of the god Vishnu) and

Arjuna in the company of Draupadi and Satyabhama (wife of Krishna and an incarnation of Bhudevi), exhilarated by *bassia* wine. In the *Harivamsa*, which is an appendix to the *Mahabharata*, Balarama, an *avatara* of Vishnu, is described as 'inflamed by plentiful libations of *kadamba* liquor' dancing with his wife. And in the *Ramayana*, Rama, an *avatara* of Vishnu, is described as embracing Sita and making her drink pure *maireya* wine. Sita, incidentally, seems to have a great fascination for wine. For while crossing the river Ganga, she promises to offer her rice cooked with meat (shall we call it biryani!) and thousands of jars of wine, and while being ferried across the Yamuna, she says that she will worship the river with a thousand cows and hundred jars of wine when her husband accomplishes his vow. The use of alcohol by the gods is not confined to the Vedic and Epic traditions. In the Puranic mythology Durga, Shiva's consort, is described as fond of wine and is invoked as *Sidhumamsapashupriya* (fond of wine, meat and animals). Similarly, Uma, also a consort of Shiva, is said to be a lover of wine and meat. In the Puranas there is the famous story of the churning of the ocean (*samudramanthan*) from which Varuni, emerged. She was the Indian goddess of wine; *varuni* was also the name of a strong liquor.

The Tantric religion is characterized by the use of five *makaras* – *madya* (wine), *mamsa* (meat), *matsya* (fish), *mudra* (gesture) and *maithuna* (sexual intercourse) – and these were offered to gods, though only the followers of Vamachara were entitled to the use of *panchamakaras* (five Ms). Much can be said about the Tantric affiliation of the goddess Kali and her various manifestations but it should suffice to refer to a goddess called Chandamari, a form of Kali and described in an eleventh century text as using human skulls as drinking vessels. In the *Kularnavatantra*, an early medieval text, it is stated that 'wine and meat are the symbols of Shakti and Shiva respectively and their consumer is Bhairava'. Not surprisingly, liquor was offered to Bhairava in early India. The practice has continued in our own times and one can see this at Bhairava temple in Delhi and at Kala Bhairava temple in Ujjain. According to a practice current in Birbhum, a 'gigantic vessel of wine is brought in front of the deity called Dharma who is carried in a procession to the house of a Sundi, who belongs to the wine making caste. In both Tantric and tribal religions the divinities are often associated with alcohol in various ways. These few examples clearly show that some gods and goddesses cherished alcohol; and their worship would remain incomplete without it.

It may be pointed out that there were a large variety of intoxicating drinks, nearly fifty types of them, available in ancient India. The use of alcohol by men was quite common, despite occasional dharmashastric objections in the case of brahmins; and instances of drinking among women was not rare. The Buddhist Jataka literature mentions many instances of drunkenness. Sanskrit literature too is replete with references to intoxicating drinks. The *Arthashastra* of Kautilya, which belongs to the Mauryan period, discusses the duties of the superintendent of *sura*; the *Charakasamhita* mentions the good and bad effects of drinking, the *Kamasutra* of Vatsyayana, and the entire corpus of the classical works including those of Kalidasa is replete with references to the use of alcohol in various contexts. A twelfth century text, *Manasollasa*, provides a graphic description of the game of drinking (*madirapanakrida*); a late Sanskrit text goes to extent of saying that, Kadambara, a juice prepared of grapes, works as a cure for erectile dysfunction. Given this background of the frequent mention of alcoholic drinks at least some Indians were certainly connoisseurs of intoxicating drinks; they were bon vivants in a sense; even today more than a thousand communities regularly indulge in drinking. If our ancestors created gods in their own image, our politicians need not be offended by divine hedonism. Prohibitionist politicians should not be indiscreet: after all, the gods are watching!

SEVEN

Historiography: From Colonial to Post-Colonial*

WE ARE LIVING in the 'the best of times' because our present rulers claim to have ushered in a New India; and we are living in the 'worst of times' because Reason has given way to Unreason; Nehru's 'tryst with destiny' in 1947 brought in 'the spring of hope', but Modi's tryst with disaster in 2014 has brought in 'the winter of despair.' In Modi's India the present is fabricated and the past is mythicized. Ignorant and goofy statements about our past are made every now and then by no less than Prime Minister Narendra Modi himself. He flies the Vedic planes though the first aeroplane is attributed to Wright brothers, who discovered it as recently as 1903; he attributes the birth of Karna to invitro fertilization of Kunti and not to her premarital *affaire d'amour*; and treats Ganesha's elephant trunk as a marvel of ancient plastic surgery performed by Shiva. In the new milieu Ashoka the Maurya

*Lecture delivered at ARSD College, University of Delhi, on 23 March 2017.

has become Ashoka the Kushwaha; the fictional Padmavati has become a real woman of ravishing beauty and the symbol of the Rajput pride and identity. One should not be surprised if some day an announcement is made from the RSS headquarters at Nagpur that Gandhi was not shot dead by Godse – he committed suicide! Historians are specially shocked when a Cambridge based archaeologist of sorts[1] with no major excavation to his credit and owing his prosperity to plagiarism, says that all Indian historians are 'rascals' and, along with some academics (most of them non-historians), dismisses the entire corpus of historical research produced by 'leftist' historians as 'legislated history'.[2] New India is then post-truth India where facts have become a taboo; where falsehoods and fabrications masquerade as facts and history has morphed into mystery. Against the background of all this it is worthwhile recalling how our colonial masters looked at our past, how anti-imperialist scholars differed with them and how the Hindutva brigade has embraced the imperialist view of pre-colonial India.

I

The British interest in the Indian history and culture began in the later half of the eighteenth century, especially after the grant of Diwani to the English East India Company in 1765. The Company's officers, inspired by the need to understand the Indian history and culture, translated Sanskrit texts like the *Manusmriti*, *Bhagvadgita* and the *Hitopadesha* into English. The best known among these officers was William Jones, a polyglot, who founded the Asiatic Society in 1784. Since then many British scholars and administrators, Charles Grant (1746-1823), James Mill (1773-1836), Montstuart Elphinstone (1779-1859), Max Müller (1823-1900) and Vincent A. Smith (1848-1920), to name only a few, wrote on the various aspects of India and its history and culture. Some of them were sympathetic to India but others were either patronizing or hostile. Therefore the corpus of literature generated by the British was not univocal. But taken together their writings created stereotypes which ideologically supported the British rule in India.

Some of the stereotypes created by the British were very widespread in the pre-Independence period and continue to remain embedded in popular consciousness even today. They are: (i) The Indian people lacked historical consciousness and did not produce any historical works which could measure up to those of the Greek historians Herodotus and Thucydides or the Roman historians Livy and Tacitus; (ii) Indian society has been changeless or static since its inception and can be changed only through British intervention; (iii) the people of the subcontinent were divided into a perpetually antagonistic Hindu and Muslim binary; this idea was anchored in the arbitrary division of Indian history by James Mill into 'Hindu' and 'Muslim' periods according to the religion of their rulers; and (iv) Indians were an otherworldly people, excessively preoccupied with religion, philosophy and spiritualism and were least concerned with the material world; this rendered them unfit to rule themselves and hence the British were justified in ruling over them.

Some Indian thinkers, writers and historians have questioned these stereotypes from time to time since the late nineteenth century, but others, writing especially during the period of the freedom struggle, seem to have either endorsed them or turned them upside down so as to create their own counter stereotypes. These have often fed into the pseudo historical views which have a striking resemblance with the clichés mentioned earlier.

II

To begin with the first stereotype, as early as eleventh century Alberuni had stated that 'the Hindus do not pay much attention to the historical order of things'.[3] This view found place in the writings of the British who generally held that ancient Indians had no historical consciousness and did not produce any work of history, except[4] the *Rajatarangini* of Kalhana (twelfth century), which chronicled the history of Kashmir.

The idea of India's ahistoricity struck deep roots in the British historical literature and became axiomatic also with most Indian historians. Even R.C. Majumdar, the most nationalist among them, asserted that India did not produce any historical work except the *Rajatarangini*. But it is surprising that neither he nor those who dittoed his view appreciated the importance of the well-known Buddhist texts like *Dipavamsa*, *Mahavamsa* and the *Vamsavalis*,[5] temple records like the *Madalapanji*, a large number of *prashastis*, and royal biographies like Bana's *Harshacharita* (seventh century),

Bilhana's *Vikramankadevacharita* (eleventh century) and Sandhyakaranandi's *Ramacharita,* and a host of other literary and commentarial works as well as the huge corpus of numismatic and epigraphic material. The number of inscriptions in India is huge, 60,000 of them being available in south India alone.[6] There is no doubt that epigraphy has been a major source of early Indian history and, according to one estimate,[7] inscriptions provide about 80 per cent of information about India before AD 1000. But despite the availability of a large body of source material it has been a common refrain among historians, including Majumdar, that there are no historical works in ancient India: One finds this extremely puzzling especially in view of the fact that they have not only used them for their own research but have also written long laudatory articles on the historical ideas in Sanskrit and Pali texts, bardic literature and coins and inscriptions.[8] Be that as it may, the accessible sources of ancient Indian history are plentiful even though they articulate a consciousness of the past which is different from what is found in contemporary historical writings.[9]

The Indian historians of the colonial and post colonial periods have heavily relied on the available sources mentioned above. Most of them have studied them uncritically but others have adopted an analytical and interdisciplinary approach. The historians of the latter category are the mainstream historians who have given direction to critical historical scholarship in the post-colonial period. They have derived much insight and information from archaeology, anthropology, ethnology, linguistics and so on. They have promoted an interaction between these disciplines and history, and have added to the diversity of sources and the nature of information derived from them. This interdisciplinarity has enabled the mainstream historians to move away from the traditional drum and trumpet history of kings and their battles, and of the fortuitous dynastic changes, and to ask new questions about the social, economic and cultural developments in early India; their focus thus shifted from the history of kings and queens to the history of the people. Through a rigorous scientific analysis of historical forces they have, on the one hand, confronted head on the imperialist historiography which denigrated the Indian civilization; and have demolished the Hindutva fantasies and fabrications about the Indian past on the other. They have thus contested the colonial stereotypes and debunked Hindutva shibboleths about Indian religion and culture.

The historical research carried out by the mainstream historians is free from xenophobic bias. It has demystified India's past and raised inconvenient questions about, religion, caste, gender, etc. But this has not gone well with the Sangh Parivar; rather it has generated a fear of history among its members.[10] The Hindutva brigade has therefore dismissed all scientific history as 'legislated history'. Interestingly, it has recently begun to ask whether we need any history at all. And, if we must need one, they tell us, the Puranas and the Epics, are good enough histories which must be swallowed as such without subjecting them to any scrutiny.[11] Thus the response of the Hindutva ideologues to the colonial view of India's supposed lack of historical records as well as to the Indian historians' rational analysis which does not unduly glorify the 'Hindu' past is identical: to do away with history altogether, much as a crazy person would cure his headache by getting his head chopped off.

III

As pointed out earlier, the second stereotype about India's supposed age-old stagnation was created by the British to justify that their rule alone could act as an agent of change in Indian society and ensure its progress. In the pre-Independence period the revivalist Indian historians, who believed in the pristine purity of Indian culture, endorsed the view that Indian culture has been changeless for centuries and took pride in the uninterrupted continuity of its culture from the beginning. This led to a frenzy among them to assign the beginning of the Indian civilization to a fantastic antiquity, some times even to the geological time. One of the earliest examples of this is provided by Bal Gangadhar Tilak (1856-1920). He pushed the date of the Vedic period from 1500 BC first to 4000 BC and then to 8000 BC, and wove 'a thread of cultural and religious continuity between the Aryans of the furthest antiquity and present-day Hindus'.[12] Another early example of pushing back the antiquity of Indian culture is found in a 1920 work by Abinash Chandra Das, lecturer in ancient Indian history and culture in Calcutta University. He argued that the Aryans were the original inhabitants of Sapta-Sindhu (modern Punjab) which, according to him, was 'the oldest life-producing region in the whole of the Indian subcontinent', and assigned the Rigvedic hymns to 25,000 years ago or the Pleistocene Age.[13] This anticipates the modern day crazy claim of the Hindutva ideologues that Hinduism is the oldest religion of the world, eternal and unchanging, and that the Hindu civilization has existed in the Ganga valley uninterruptedly since 1972 million years[14] which is millions of years before the Jurassic age.

The post-Independence historians, some of whom are of Marxist persuasion, have proved the absurdity of such ideas as those of Tilak, Das and of the votaries of Hindutva. They have not only rejected the ridiculous dating of the Vedas or 'Hindu' civilization but, have also repudiated the idea of its supposed changelessness.

In critiquing the notion of the supposed immutability of Indian society the Indian historians have identified the elements of change and continuity in Indian society; some of them, though influenced by Marxism, have demonstrated the flaws of even Marx's perception of Indian society as stagnant. This is evident from their critical engagement with the notion of Oriental Despotism as well as Karl Marx's theory of the Asiatic Mode of Production. Both these constructs are inextricably linked,[15] and presuppose the existence of a static society, absence of private property in land and state's absolute control over agrarian resources, especially irrigation. The Indian Marxist historians, through a critical examination of the empirical data, have however, demonstrated that the Indian society has registered major changes in all spheres of life including social structure, landownership patterns and social distribution of land, trade and urbanization, nature of state, religious beliefs and practices and art and architecture, etc. They have thus proved that these two constructs are untenable, and hence inapplicable to India.[16]

But in total disregard of the analytical and credible historical literature produced during the last seven decades or so, the Hindutva ideologues have continued to relentlessly propagate that the Indian (Hindu in their lexicon!) civilization is the oldest civilization of the world, eternal and immutable, and has remained unchanged since its inception. They have thus remained stuck to the British/ Western idea of a stagnant India. Instead of identifying the elements of change and continuity, which form the central theme of scientific history, they are engaged in a perpetual battle for greater antiquity and longer period of changelessness of Indian society and culture. The Hindutva enthusiasts who favour a fanciful antiquity of the 'Hindu' civilization are also proud of their supposed direct descent from the Aryans whom they consider the original inhabitants of India and whose imagined greatness is a constant refrain among the members of the Sangh Parivar. They forget that the idea of Aryan glory and greatness is not of Indian origin but is borrowed from the foreigners who wrote in colonial times.

It was, in fact, Friedrich Max Müller, who first spoke of the Aryan foundation of Indian culture. His view was shared by Col. Olcott (1832-1907) and Madame Blavatsky (1831-91). Of these the first was a German born philologist and Orientalist, and a naturalized citizen of England who never visited India but Sanskritized his name as Moksa

Mula (could it be that this has inspired the American mascot of Hindutva, David Frawley, to become Vamadeva Shastri!); the second was an American military officer and the first president of the Theosophical Society founded in 1875 and the third, its co-founder, was a Russian occultist. These three earliest exponents of the Aryan greatness, however, had different views on the issue of the original home of the Aryans. Max Müller postulated the migration of the Aryans from the north-west into India while the two theosophists asserted that the Aryans were indigenous to India. In their view the Aryan culture was the cradle of civilization, and spread from India to the West and different parts of the world.

Like the theosophists, Dayananda Saraswati (1824-83), who founded the Arya Samaj in 1875, considered the Aryans as indigenous and the Vedas as repository of all knowledge and wisdom. The Arya Samaj merged with the Theosophical Society which also was founded in 1875. Though this merger did not last long they never differed on the Aryan question. The Right wing idologues have adhered to the view of the theosophists and Dayananda and have some times gone to ridiculous lengths. One can see this in the writings of Golwalkar who tries to reconcile his own view of Aryan indigenism with Tilak's theory of Aryan migration. Tilak, as is well known, had asserted (1903) that the Aryan homeland was in the North Pole. Golwalkar (1947), who could not have the courage to disregard his view, made the absurd and laughable assertion that the North Pole was not actually stationary and quite long back it was situated in what is today Bihar and Orissa!

IV

The Hindutva enthusiasts who argue for the antiquity and autochthony of their Aryan ancestors claim them to be the first inhabitants of India and hence its real masters. For them the Muslims are the 'Other' and the idea of a rigid Hindu-Muslim binary is their foundational premise, derived from the division of Indian history into Hindu and Muslim periods – a division based on the religion of the ruling dynasties.

As is well known, the division of Indian history into Hindu and Muslim periods was first introduced by the Utilitarian thinker James Mill in his *History of British India* (1823). He never visited India; nor did he know any of its languages. But his work became very influential because it was used as a prescribed reading at institutions like the Haileybury College where the English officers received their training before coming to India. His artificial division of Indian history sought to drive a wedge between the Hindus and Muslims and thus sowed the seeds of communal historiography in India. His periodization received much support from the colonial historians like H.M. Eliot and John Dawson. Their eight volumes of the *History of India as Told by its Own Historians* (1867-77), comprised faulty and biased translations of medieval Persian chronicles. The work overstated the dark side of Muslim rule, with the clear intent of inflaming passions between the Hindus and Muslims, which was in keeping with the British imperial policy, especially after 1857.

Mill's chronological scheme became widely accepted through the works of subsequent British writers, especially

Vincent Smith. It remained entrenched in Indian historical writings throughout the colonial period and has continued to influence historical studies in the Indian universities in our own time. Many Indian historians have tried to either distance themselves or break away from this periodization, or more frequently have rendered it irrelevant by focusing on historical themes which transcend strict chronological barriers. But unlike them, the scholars of Hindutva affiliation have clung oddly to the communal division of Indian history. For it supports their view that the Muslims, whose *punyabhumi* (holy land) is not India, are the 'Other'. At the political level it is thus linked with the development of communal politics in India, and the two-nation theory leading to the Partition of India, which found enthusiastic support from the Hindu nationalist V.D. Savarkar and historian R.C. Majumdar. The latter famously said that during the Turkish sultanate 'for the first time in Indian history, two distinct but important communities [Hindus and Muslims] and cultures stood face to face, and India was permanently divided into two powerful units'. It is this kind of statement which dubs Muslims as foreigners and inspires many people including Prime Minister Modi to speak of 1,200 years of foreign rule in India.

The Hindutva claim that the Hindus and their supposed ancestors, the Aryans, are the original inhabitants of India, has meant that they are the progenitors of the oldest Indian civilization, which is the Harappan. But some of its important centres (e.g. Mohenjo Daro and Harappa) are situated in Pakistan, so its roots must be found in India. Not surprisingly many onomastics enthusiasts have named the Harappan civilization after the river Saraswati. Thus one can immediately see the link between the communal periodization, depiction of Muslims as foreigners and the naming of the Harappan civilization after the mythical river Saraswati.

The general acceptance of Mill's periodization has another significant implication. It has led many Indian historians, especially those writing during the freedom movement, to indulge in an uncritical glorification of the 'Hindu' and severe denigration of the 'Muslim' periods. Examples of this are many but a few of them may be mentioned here: the Vedas are the repositories of all knowledge; the Mauryan monarchy as reflected in the *Arthashastra* of Kautilya was as good as the British constitutional monarchy; ancient Indian tribal oligarchies were like Athenian democracy;[17] the village *sabhas* in south India were little village democracies;[18] and the Gupta period was the golden age. The nationalist historians thus looked at the entire 'Hindu' period as one of affluence, social harmony and happiness and of great cultural achievements – a cloud-cuckoo-land if ever there was one! Their ideas provided an ideological weapon to the freedom fighters who, living in a state of dystopia as it were, were looking for a utopia in the past. In Independent India, however, the stereotypes created by the nationalists have been shown to be without basis. They have become irrelevant and redundant and have been justly jettisoned by the mainstream historians. They have, however, survived as the hobbyhorses of those who fly Vedic planes and drive Vedic motor cars.

V

The fourth colonial stereotype about Indians was that they were otherworldly people, given so much to spiritual activities that they were unable to govern themselves. The British used it to justify their own rule in India, but the Indian scholars embraced the idea so as to project India as the spiritual preceptor of the world. It is true that Indians made significant contribution to science, philosophy and literature in the ancient period which influenced the development of ideas in other parts of the world. In modern times, their influence is seen in the ideas of many thinkers and writers including poets like Herder and philosophers like Schopenhauer.[19]

But the Indian influence abroad was very often blown out of proportion and India was projected as a civilizer of other countries, especially those in South-East Asia. It was against this background that a group of Calcutta based scholars including the linguist Suniti Kumar Chatterjee and historians P.C. Bagchi, Kali Das Nag and Ramesh Chandra Majumdar founded the Greater India Society in 1926 under the patronage of Rabindranath Tagore.[20] Of them Majumdar emerged as the most vocal supporter of the Greater India paradigm and claimed that the Hindu colonists 'transplanted' their whole culture and civilization among the South-East Asian peoples 'who had not yet emerged from their primitive barbarism'.[21]

But soon the Indianization thesis came to be questioned by a young Dutch scholar, J.E. van Leur, who published his work in 1934 and since then a rich corpus of literature has been published in favour of an autonomous history of South-East Asia. But the notion of the so-called Hindu colonies continues to inspire the foot soldiers of Indian jingoism who take pride in India's 'supposed imperialist past'. It is reminiscent of the pan-Germanism of the Nazis and supports the Akhand Bharat project of those who aspire to 'reinstall India as the teacher of the world'.[22] It would thus appear from the above that the ideas glorifying early India, which provided ideological support to the freedom struggle, are being used as building blocks of a historiography which seeks to perpetuate the colonial perception of India as ahistorical, stagnant, otherworldly, and riven by Hindu-Muslim antagonism.

NOTES

1. Dilip Kumar Chakrabarti in an interview to the *Statesman* Calcutta, 6 Feruary 2016.
2. *The Hindu*, 17 November 2015.
3. *Alberuni's India*, London, 1910, vol. II, p. 10.
4. A.A. Macdonell went to the extent of making a belittling statement that 'early India wrote no history because it never made any': *History of Sanskrit Literature*, London, 1900, p. 11.
5. Michael Witzel, 'On Indian Historical Writing: The Role of the Vamsavalis', *Journal of the Japanese Association for South Asian Studies*, vol. 2, 1990, pp. 1-57.
6. According to Noboru Karashima the number of inscriptions may be around 60,000 in south India alone. *The Past as Known from Tamil Inscriptions:* https://f.hypotheses.org/wpcontent/blogs.dir/439/files/2012/05/Karashima_paper_toronto_2012.pdf.

7. Richard Salomon, *Indian Epigraphy: A Guide to the Study of Inscriptions in Sanskrit, Prakrit, and the Other Indo-Aryan Languages*, New York, 1998, p. 3.
8. C.H. Philips, ed., *Historians of India, Pakistan and Ceylon*, London, 1961.
9. Romila Thapar has convincingly refuted the alleged ahistoricity of ancient India through a series of articles culminating in her landmark publication *The Past Before Us*, Delhi, 2013.
10. S. Gopal, 'The Fear of History', *Seminar*, no. 221, January 1978.
11. For a recent discussion on the relevance/irrevalence of history see S.N. Balgangadhar, 'What do Indians Need: A History or the Past', http://www.hipkapi.com/2012/02/16/what-do-indians-need-a-history-or-the-past-s-n-balagangadhara/; Rajan Gurukkal, 'A Blindness About India', *Economic and Political Weekly,* Vol XLIX, no. 49, 6 December 2014; Romila Thapar, 'India: Fallacies of Hindutva Historiography', *Economic and Political Weekly*, vol. L, no. 1, 3 January 2015.
12. Vasant Kaiwar, 'The Aryan Model of History and the Oriental Renaissance: The Politics of Identity in an Age of Revolutions, Colonialism and Nationalism', in Vasant Kaiwar and Sucheta Mazumdar, eds., *Antinomies of Modernity: Essays on Race, Orient, Nation*, Delhi, 2003, p. 45. Tilak discussed these issues in his *Orion or Researches into the Antiquity of the Vedas*, Bombay, 1893; and *The Arctic Home in the Vedas*, Bombay, 1903.
13. A.C. Das, *Rgvedic India*, Calcutta, 1971 [1920], pp. 22-3.
14. https://apnabhaarat.wordpress.com/what-is-a-relegion/hinduism/
15. The origins of the concept of Oriental Despotism can be traced to Aristotelian political thought. It has shaped the European perception of Asiatic polity and society over the centuries and has played a significant role in the philosophy of several western thinkers. It formed the basis of Karl Marx's concept of the Asiatic Mode of Production which was rejected in 1931 by the Leningrad Conference held under the auspices of Stalin. But it was resurrected in 1957 by Karl Wittfogel in his *Oriental Despotism: A Comparative Study of Total Power* which triggered a fresh debate on the nature of Asian, especially Indian society.

16. The debate on Oriental Despotism and Asiatic Mode of Production was initiated by Damodar Dharmanand Kosambi with his scathing review of Karl Wittfogel's *Oriental Despotism*, New Haven, 1957 soon after its publication. It has continued for more than three decades in which Irfan Habib, S.N. Mukherjee, Bipan Chandra, R.S. Sharma and Romila Thapar have participated at different times. (See Kosambi 'The Basis of Despotism', *Economic Weekly*, vol. IX, no. 44, 2 November 1957, pp. 1417-19; Irfan Habib, 'An Examination of Wittfogel's Theory of Oriental Despotism', *Enquiry*, no. 6, Old Series, 1962, pp. 54-73; Mukherjee, 'The Idea of the Village Community and the British Administrators', *Enquiry*, New Series, III, no. 3 (Winter 1971), pp. 57-67; Bipan Chandra, 'Karl Marx, His Theories of Asian Societies and Colonial Rule', *Review*, 5 (Summer 1981), 13-91; R.S. Sharma, 'The Social Economic Bases of "Oriental Despotism" in Early India', *Essays in Honour of Dr. Gyanchand*, ed. S.K. Bose, New Delhi, 1981.)
17. K.P. Jaiswal, *Hindu Polity*, Calcutta, 1924.
18. K.A. Nilakanta Sastri, *The Colas*, Madras University, 1935; idem, *A History of South India*, New Delhi, 1955.
19. Benoy Kumar Sarkar, 'The Influence of India on Western Civilization in Modern Times', *The Journal of Race Development*, vol. 9, no. 1 (July 1918), pp. 91-104.
20. For a detailed discussion see Susan Bayly, 'Imaginning "Greater India": French and Indian Visions of Colonialism in the Indic Mode', *Modern Asian Sudies*, vol. 38, no. 3 (July 2004), pp. 703-44.
21. R.C. Majumdar, *Greater India*, Sholapur, 1940, p. 21, cited Hermann Kulke, 'Early State Formation and "Indianization": Reflections on the Concept of Convergence', in N. Karashima, ed., *Medieval Religious Movements and Social Change*, Tokyo, 2016, p. 158.
22. *Indian Express*, 5 June 2015.

EIGHT

Damodar Dharmanand Kosambi: Father of Scientific Indian History*

BORN ON 31 JULY 1907 at Kosben in Goa, Damodar Dharmanand Kosambi was the son of Dharmanand Kosambi, the reputed Buddhist scholar who taught at Harvard for several years and from whom Damodar Kosambi, known as Baba to his friends, inherited his passion for learning, his sharp versatile intellect, and above all his humanism. After some schooling in Pune he accompanied his father to the United States and studied at the Cambridge Latin School until 1925. In 1929 he graduated with brilliant results from the Harvard University, where he showed special interest and proficiency in mathematics, history and several languages, especially Greek, Latin, German and French. During his stay at Harvard Kosambi was in contact with distinguished

*Reprinted from D.N. Jha, ed., *The Many Careers of D.D. Kosambi*, Delhi, 2011.

mathematicians such as George Birkhoff and Norbert Wiener.

On his return to India in 1929 Kosambi joined the mathematics faculty of the Banaras Hindu University, where he produced a group of competent researchers. Before long he emerged as a mathematician of outstanding ability and was invited by the Aligarh Muslim University, where he taught for a year. In 1932 he decided to settle down at Pune as professor of mathematics at the Fergusson College, where his father had taught Pali for several years before he went to Harvard. During the fourteen years that Kosambi taught at the Fergusson College he incessantly tried to master various fields of knowledge and established himself as a great scholar and thinker of modern India. In 1946 he was offered the Chair of mathematics at the Tata Institute of Fundamental Research, Bombay, a position that he held till 1962. There he was able to interact with scholars of equal calibre from all over the world.

II

D.D. Kosambi specialized in and taught mathematics during most of his teaching career, and his contribution to this area has been acclaimed by many experts including the famous British scientist J.D. Bernal, who as much lauded his scientific works as his role in the world peace movement. The present writer is in no position to assess the importance of his researches in the sciences; but he certainly broke traditional disciplinary boundaries and made valuable, lasting and socially relevant contributions to genetics, statistics and other branches of knowledge. In genetics his work on chromosome mapping (1944) was believed to be an advance on the prevalent chromosome theory. In statistics he developed a powerful technique of data analysis called Proper Orthogonal Decomposition (POD).[1] At the invitation of the Academia Sinica, he visited Beijing where, in his discussion with Kuo-Mo-Jo and Chou En-Lai, he suggested statistical methods for the forecasting of Chinese food crops and quality control in industry. At home, he forcefully argued against the arbitrary location and construction of dams and suggested statistical methods for the purpose. Similarly his study of the seasonal death rate proved that at least 500 lives could be saved annually in the city of Bombay alone by concentrating on anti-typhoid work about three weeks before the onset of the monsoon. He also suggested to the then Bombay government that a motorable all-weather road for Naneghat would be far more economical than the proposed expensive funicular.

Kosambi was far from being an ivory tower scholar. His intellectual activity was deeply rooted in and greatly inspired by the needs of the people around him. Not surprisingly, he expressed himself fearlessly on issues of national and international importance. For example, more than half a century before the Indian government mortgaged its sovereignty to the USA by signing a nuclear agreement with it, he asserted that India 'is too poor a country to throw money away on costly fads like atomic energy merely because they look modern' and was passionately pleading for solar rays as an alternative source of energy.[2]

III

Often described as a man of truly 'Renaissance versatility' D.D. Kosambi applied his abstract mathematical methods to the study of various branches of social sciences. He thus extended the statistical method to the study of punch-marked coins and, by weighing nearly 12,000 coins (including 7,000 modern ones), he laid the foundation of scientific numismatics in India.[3] He established a link between the king-lists in the Pali Buddhist works on the one hand and the marks on the punch-marked coins on the other and ascribed them to the rulers of Magadha and Kosala. His method of dating the coins was seriously inhibited by his disregard for their archaeological stratigraphic context, but, proceeding on the assumption that every coin bears the signature of contemporary society, he tried to fix the chronology of punch-marked coins and postulated the relevance of the two famous Taxila coin hoards (dominated by the Magadhan issues) to the economic history of Taxila as well as Magadha. Unlike the numismatists who wrote before and after him, Kosambi not only rescued numismatics from the coin collectors' purely antiquarian interest but also emphasized their importance for the reconstruction of the social and economic history of India. Accordingly he was the first to refer to the paucity of coinage and to its linkage with the decline of trade and the emergence of the self sufficient village economy in the post-Gupta period. The quantitative method which he applied to the study of the earliest Indian coins has not had any takers, but more or less at the same time as he published his paper on scientific numismatics, R.S. Sharma pointed to some of its limitations, made a strong case for the study of early Indian monetary history,[4] and himself undertook in-depth studies of the paucity of coinage, the decline of trade and urban centres, and the growth of the self-sufficient village economy, all these later becoming the building blocks of his model of 'Indian feudalism' and the characteristic features of what is now known as the early medieval period in Indian history.

IV

From the examination of ancient coin groups, Kosambi proceeded to ask who issued them. Struck by 'the shocking discordance' of the written sources (e.g. the Puranas, Buddhist and Jain records) which 'give different names for the same king', he decided to go to the original texts himself, for which he needed a mastery of Sanskrit. Despite his uncharacteristically modest statement that he 'absorbed Sanskrit only through the pores without a regular study',[5] he appears to have turned almost instinctively to his Sanskrit inheritance and acquired unquestionable proficiency in Sanskrit, Pali and Prakrit through having worked with his father, and in association with V.S. Sukthankar. His grasp over Sanskrit was indeed remarkable; it ranged from his interest in the search for manuscripts to their editing and publication. His critical editions of Bhartrihari's *Shatakatraya* (1942),

Chintamanisharanika of Dashabala (1949), Vidyakara's *Subhashitaratnakosha* (1957), as well as his writings on the *Parvasamgraha* of the *Mahabharata* (1946) and the text of the *Arthashastra* (1958) are lasting testimony to Kosambi's mastery of Sanskrit as well as his attainments in the field of text literary criticism. His translation (done jointly with J.L. Masson) of Bhasa's drama *Avimaraka* (1970) is also evidence of his linguistic competence in Sanskrit. In the later years of his life Kosambi was engaged in a standard translation of the *Arthashastra* of Kautilya, a project he could not complete on account of his sudden death on 29 June 1966.

Of the works examined and edited by D.D. Kosambi, the best known are Bhartrihari's *Shatakatraya* and Vidyakara's *Subhashitaratnakosha*. His critical edition of *Shatakatraya* is also a landmark in text criticism. On the basis of a comparative examination of 377 manuscripts out of the conservatively estimated total of 3,000 surviving manuscripts – 'undoubtedly a larger number than has ever been used for any single text in the history of Indian literary criticism'[6] – he identified 200 poems on which enough manuscripts agreed closely enough to be attributed to Bhartrihari.[7] Not surprisingly, his work has been hailed as 'a decided advance over anything his contemporaries had achieved' and 'will remain definitive for many, many more decades to come'.[8] Unlike the *Shatakatraya*, which had to be reconstructed from a large number of manuscripts, the restoration of the text of the *Subhashitaratnakosha*, an anthology prepared by Vidyakara, in a Buddhist monastery of the Pala period and dated to around AD 1100, had to be done on the basis of only three partial manuscripts, though many poems in it are drawn from other manuscripts and later anthologies.[9] The list of poets whose poems are included here mentions as many as 223; of them, Kosambi claims to have 'rescued over fifty poets from the total oblivion to which lovers of Sanskrit had consigned them'.[10] Although Daniel Ingalls, the translator of the anthology, was later to suggest more than 200 changes in the reconstructed text, according to Sheldon Pollock, Kosambi's *Subhashitaratnakosha* 'stands as one of the most valuable works in the history of Sanskrit philology'.[11]

Kosambi's analysis and understanding of Sanskrit literature was informed by his commitment to a social and political ideology rooted in Marxism. In his view, literature, like science, should be understood as a function of the age in which it is produced. He tells us 'the great poet in a class society must not only express the position and aspirations of an important class, but must also transcend the class barriers, whether explicitly or implicitly' and, to be sure, his most provocative statements on Sanskrit language and literature were about its class character – statements he made in the context of the works of both Bhartrihari and Vidyakara. Writing about the former he asserts that 'the literary physiognomy' of Bhartrihari is that of 'a hungry Brahmin in distress', whose frustrations were shared by the 'the miserable class' of brahmins. He is

> the poet of his class. But he is not a poet of the people. The Indian poets who made a real and lasting place for themselves in the hearts of the people came from the people themselves,

and not from this narrow helpless substratum shut off from the masses by birth, training, occupation or the lack of it, language and culture. Those poets spoke the languages of the people, addressed themselves to the people and not to the court. Every child knows their names and every peasant their songs – Kabir, Tukarama, Tulasidasa: what portion of the country did not possess its poet of the sort?[12]

Kosambi's stress on the class character of Sanskrit literature is also evident from his introduction to the *Subhashitaratnakosha*:

the average Sanskrit poet wrote for the patrician – we have to deal here with *class* literature. When drawing conclusions about life in ancient India from any such work as this, it must always be remembered that that life was not shared by most Indians of the poet's time or of any other time; in essence not even by the poet himself. The Sanskrit stanza implies mind and memory not otherwise preoccupied, simple leisure to work out its double and triple meanings, mythological allusions, complicated figures of speech – apart from the long training needed to write even the simplest bit of Sanskrit. The Brahmin class is primarily responsible for keeping both ritual and language alive while regarding itself as superior to the rest of the people.[13]

One may, however, find it difficult to accept that Sanskrit literature was wholly the creation of brahmins or remained solely in their possession. The earliest known mention of the great poet Bhartrihari is by the Jaina Somadevasuri in his *Yashastilakachampu* (AD 959); the oldest reference to any specific work by him, Kosambi himself tells us, is in the *Prabandhachintamani* (AD 1306) of the famous Jaina Acarya Merutunga; and the first commentary on Bhartrihari's *Shatakatraya*, so ably edited by Kosambi, was written by a Jaina called Dhanasara in around 1478 at Jaipur. Similarly, the author of the anthology *Subhashita-ratnakosha*, whose text was reconstructed by Kosambi himself, was Vidyakara, an abbot of the Buddhist monastery at Jaggadala during the Pala period. Even the author of the astrological text *Chintamanisharanika* was a Buddhist called Dashabala. All this shows that Sanskrit was not the monopoly of the brahmins and that it was very much the idiom used by Buddhists and Jainas. But this does not contradict Kosambi's basic assertion about the class character of Sanskrit literature; for the Jaina and Buddhist authors writing in Sanskrit were neither indigent nor were they totally deprived of patronage: the Jaina Acharya Hemachandra (eleventh-twelfth century) is a case in point. There is thus much truth in the view that classical Sanskrit literature was the literature of the upper class, though it is not hard to find the description of poverty and misery in it. Vidyakara, verse 1318, for example, reads: 'Naked as I am my skin must play the cloak, a cloak well furred with gooseflesh raised by the cold wind'.[14]

The use of historical materialism in reading literature and analysing it from the class perspective is also seen in Kosambi's study of the working class in the *Amarakosha*. Its author Amarasimha was 'mnemonically superior' to other lexicographers because 'he gave more attention to objective reality than to ideal categories' and so gives a good idea of social divisions. Kosambi therefore undertakes an elaborate analysis of terms in the text that are related to the working class, which leads him to state that 'the

Amarakosha was written in feudal times', although he is conscious that 'the evidence is poor'.[15] Another important example of Kosambi's interpretation of literature against its changing social contexts is his essay on the Urvashi-Pururvas story which travels a long distance in time from its earliest occurrences in the *Rigveda* and *Shatapatha Brahmana* to become the theme of the five-act drama *Vikramorvashiyam* written by Kalidasa. Kosambi analyses the original version of the myth as well as its variations found in various literary texts over time, and argues how Kalidasa's retelling of it 'reflects the difference between the Vedic society and the Gupta period, being in fact a transition from ritual to drama'.[16] Kosambi applies a similar approach to the *Bhagvadgita*. 'The song divine,' he tells us, 'is sung for the upper classes by the Brahmins, and only through them for others.' He also links the *bhakti* doctrine enunciated in the *Gita* with the rise of feudalism and asserts that to hold a feudal society and state together, 'the best religion is one which emphasises the role of *bhakti*, personal faith, even though the object of devotion may have clearly visible flaws.'[17] Examples of similar studies by Kosambi may be multiplied further and, even if one may differ on details, it is difficult to reject his perception of the inherent linkage between the material conditions of society and the historical prevalence of specific literary and aesthetic forms.[18]

V

While D.D. Kosambi underscored the importance of scientific numismatic studies and class analysis of literature, he was equally aware of the utility of archaeology for the reconstruction of the Indian past and did much valuable archaeological work himself. He discovered megaliths in the Poona district, collected a huge amount of microliths and, on the basis of his finds, tried to explain the movements of ancient peoples and establish prehistoric links between the Deccan and central India. His field work led also to the discovery of ancient trade routes, Buddhist caves at Kuda, and some ancient inscriptions which he published along with his own comments. Kosambi undertook archaelogical explorations more than half a century ago and, not surprisingly, some of his conclusions appear dated, flawed and unacceptable now, but the trashing of his archaeology by Shereen Ratnagar,[19] a reputed Indian archaeologist, on the ground that he did not publish his findings in the bulletins of the Archaeological Survey of India (e.g. *Indian Archaeology: A Review* and *Ancient India*) and in any peer reviewed journal is an amusing academic trivia – that his writings appeared in the *Man,* published by the Royal Anthropological Institute of England and Ireland is of no consequence to her! She has also pointed out that by the 1960s the faculty of the Deccan College, Poona (of which her mentor H.D. Sankalia was the director) had excavated several sites from Rajasthan to northern Karnataka, but Kosambi wilfully ignored the data available from them.[20] While one may find fault with both Sankalia and Kosambi in their soured personal relationship which prevented any fruitful academic interaction between them, one cannot ignore the fact that Indian archaeologists (Sankalia included) have not been forthcoming in sharing their data with the scholarly community outside their respective caucuses; and, suffering from an antiquity frenzy as they do, they have generally shied away from thinking of larger issues of social and cultural transformation. Nor can one disregard the fact that several reports of the sites excavated by the Deccan College were published only a few months before Kosambi's demise so that he could not possibly have seen them. One of them saw the light of the day no less than three years after his death. It is preposterous therefore to allege that Kosambi disregarded the data available in his time. His review of Sankalia's *Prehistory and Protohistory in India and Pakistan* (Bombay, 1962-3), which incorporated data from all the sites excavated by Sankalia and his colleagues, albeit harsh and unkind, does take notice of what could have been the latest excavated material available at the time.[21] Also, it is necessary to bear in mind that Kosambi shared neither the obsessive antiquarianism of the Indian archaeologists nor their rigid adherence to Mortimer Wheeler's perception that the sole purpose of archaeology was to identify stratigraphies, which could serve as chronometer of culture sequences but could not address Kosambi's concern with larger historical issues and with factors of social, economic and cultural change – a concern that did not find place in the agenda of the so-called 'trained' archaeologists at all and even today gets limited attention from them. In his view, Indian archaeology had 'achieved nothing of correlative historical value'[22] and was not 'advanced enough to solve the really important questions, not even to ask some of them'.[23] He asserted that a meaningful use of archaeological material was possible only if it was correlated not just with the traditional written records but also with ethnographic data which offers a detailed analysis of phenomena roughly comparable to those which the historians are reconstructing with a good deal less evidence. This meant extensive field work and collection of anthropological data including folklore, oral traditions and myths which furnish clues to aspects of human life forgotten over time. He himself undertook field studies with 'critical insight, taking nothing for granted or on faith', and gathered substantial evidence to support his archaeological data, to confirm the historical process of mutual acculturation between tribal and caste-based agrarian societies, as well as to trace the tribal origins of many Hindu deities, religious beliefs and practices, and thus demystified Indian history and philosophy. The archaeological method of Kosambi was vastly enriched by ethnographic material whose neglect, he tells us, 'leads to a ridiculous distortion of Indian history and to a misunderstanding of Indian culture, not compensated by subtle theology or the boasts of having risen above crass materialism'.[24] His archaeology, despite its limitations, may be the precursor of what is nowadays fashionably called ethnoarchaeology just as his historical work introduced into Indian historiography an interdisciplinary approach[25] which is nowadays more often talked about than practised.

VI

Combining his understanding of historical materialism with an interdisciplinary method, D.D. Kosambi undertook extensive researches on various aspects of Indian history and culture,[26] which appeared in the form of more than a hundred articles from the early 1940s onwards. He later wove his major findings into the three books: *Introduction to the Study of Indian History* (1956), *Myth and Reality* (1962) and *Culture and Civilisation of Ancient India in Historical Outline* (1965). Written in a highly effective style, with occasional acerbity, his works were a strong antidote to the colonial pontification about and the nationalist glorification of the Indian past; and stirred the stagnant and turgid waters of contemporary Indian historiography.

That Kosambi made use of Marxism in his researches on Indian history is clear from his oft quoted statement: 'History is the presentation in chronological order of successive changes in the means and relations of production.' However, he disapproved of the application of 'a mechanical determinism, particularly in dealing with India'.[27] Marxism, he said, is 'far from the economic determinism which its opponents so often take it to be'.[28] It 'cannot be reduced to a rigid formalism like mathematics' and 'cannot be treated a standard technique such as an automobile lathe'. It was for him a method, 'a tool of analysis', and not 'a substitute for thinking'. Accordingly Kosambi did not hesitate even to reject some of the formulations of Marx and Engels if they did not fit facts. In his view the history of India could not be straightjacketed into the slavery-feudalism-capitalism scheme of periodization.[29] Not surprisingly, he asserts that ancient Indian society, unlike the Greek and the Roman, was not based on the slave mode of production. Although some people were not free from earliest times to the present century, he holds that the importance of chattel slavery in the relations of productions as a supply of labour for economic production was negligible in ancient India. The place of the slave whose surplus could be appropriated was taken by the lowest caste, that of the shudras, whom he equated with the helots of Sparta.[30] Kosambi's statement is true of the Vedic period, when slaves were few in number and could not have engaged in productive activities like their Homeric counterparts. The Vedic passages referring to the gift of slaves to priests invariably speak of women slaves, who may have worked as domestic slaves and whose participation in economic production may have been inhibited largely by the incipient nature of the agricultural economy during a major part of the Vedic period. But during the period 400-100 BC, represented by the early Pali texts and the *Arthashastra* of Kautilya, which make copious references to slaves – the latter even laying down detailed rules about them – slavery emerged as a factor in production. The Pali works, the oldest of which cannot be taken beyond 400 BC, indicate that in north-eastern India slaves (*dasas*) and hired labourers (*karmakaras*) were employed in cultivation, especially in large-sized fields ranging from 500 to 1000 *karisas*. This is confirmed by Kautilya, who enjoins the superintendent of agriculture to requisition the services of *dasas* and *karmakaras* for working on state farms. Thus there is little doubt that slaves participated in the community's productive activities during the post-Vedic and Maurya times. But even if the state and some members of society owned slaves who were made to work in the agricultural sector, it is difficult to characterize Indian society as a slave society in the absence of any quantitative data about their numerical strength. The numbers of slaves have been worked out for some other countries (e.g. classical Athens, Roman Italy, the West Indian Islands and southern states of the USA)[31]but this has not been done for India. Kosambi thus seems to have a point when he rejects the concept of a slave mode of production as being applicable to India.[32]

Kosambi is also critical of the Marxian notion of the Asiatic mode of production.[33] Never clearly defined by Marx and often put to highly tendentious use by Western scholars (e.g. Karl Wittfogel), his idea of the Asiatic system of production is based on the concept of a society characterized by tribal communal ownership of land and a self-sustaining economy based on a 'combination of manufacture and agriculture within the small community'. Connected with this is the view of both Marx and Engels about the slow-moving character of Oriental society, as can be inferred from the former's prominent reference to its 'stagnatory and vegetative life' and the latter's remarks on its 'tremendous staying power'. Kosambi made a departure from this orthodox Marxist notion of 'the unchangeableness of Asiatic societies'. After all, the very formation of the village economy with the plough used on a fixed plot of land implied a tremendous advance in the means of production. Self-sufficiency, which, according to the founders of Marxism, is the hallmark of Asiatic societies, was not possible in the strict sense of the term.

For, as Kosambi rightly tells us, most of the Indian villages produce neither salt nor metals, the two essentials that had to be obtained by exchange. In the years before and after his death, other historians (notably R.S. Sharma) have also questioned the supposed stagnant nature of Indian society and have drawn attention to the dispersal of agriculture, technological changes, stages in the growth of urbanization and trade and to the formation of the state from the later Vedic period down to the time of the Gupta rulers.[34] Nevertheless, it does remain true, according to Kosambi, that the Indian village tended to become nearly self-contained from the Gupta period onwards owing mainly to the decline of trade and urban centres. This led to the break-up of the guilds of merchants and artisans, who migrated to villages where they eked out a living by catering to the needs of the people and altered the rural social structure, especially through the formation of new castes. In view of the fact that Kosambi referred to some of the features of the major social transformation in early India, he does not seem to have accepted the idea of the Asiatic mode unreservedly.[35]

VII

Although Kosambi does not accept the notions of the slave and the Asiatic modes of production, he does make use of the concept of feudalism in the context of pre-colonial India. But here also he differs from the Marxist position in that he postulates two stages in the development of feudalism in India – feudalism from above and feudalism from below. The first is a 'state wherein an emperor or powerful king levied tribute from subordinates who still ruled in their own right and did what they liked within their own territories – as long as they paid the paramount ruler.' These subordinate rulers might even be tribal chiefs, and they seem in general to have ruled the land by direct administration, without the intermediacy of a class which was in effect a land-owning stratum. By feudalism from below is meant the next stage, where 'a class of landowners developed within the village, between the state and the peasantry, gradually to wield armed power over the local population'. Such two-stage feudalism has nowhere been visualized in the writings of Marx and Engels, and it has been questioned by several scholars.[36] R.S. Sharma, for example, presented overwhelming empirical data in his comprehensive work on Indian feudalism which contradicts Kosambi's model.[37] While Sharma's own work has generated animated academic debate, Kosambi's two-stage theory of feudalism has not received the attention it deserves. Be that as it may, the major weakness of the models of Indian feudalism delineated by both Kosambi or Sharma, lies in the fact that they explain feudal developments in terms of the decline of trade which depended on external factors. Essentially Pirennian[38] in nature, this explanation would in fact imply that the early Indian society did not possess any built-in potential for change – a position implicit in the theory of the Asiatic mode. But this does not go well with Kosambi's own view of caste as a class, albeit 'at a primitive level of production';

for a class society is bound to have its own contradictions which will usher in a new mode of production – in the present case, the feudal mode.

In an assessment of Kosambi's contributions to Indology, especially his views on the Indian version of feudalism, Romila Thapar has asserted that he was not familiar with the writings of Marc Bloch and Fernand Braudel, who were the founders and prominent exponents of the Annales school of historiography. Nor was Kosambi, it is further alleged, familiar with the works of Karl Polanyi.[39] The implication of her argument is that had he been familiar with the works of these scholars, he would either have viewed the feudal phenomenon differently or would not have posited its existence at all. But the criticism is unfounded. Marc Bloch's *La Societe Feodale* first appeared in French in 1939 and its English version (*Feudal Society*, 2 vols.) appeared as late as 1961, five years after Kosambi published his *Introduction to the Study of Indian History*. Braudel's famous work on the Mediterranean world was published in French in 1949 and its English version came out in 1972, more than a decade and a half after Kosambi's *Introduction.* Similarly, of the two works of Polanyi, the one which could have had some bearing on Kosambi's study of early medieval society was *Trade and Markets in Early Empires*, which was first published in 1957, a year later than Kosambi's work. Chronology thus goes against Thapar. The English versions of the French works came out after Kosambi published his own work in 1956; and one of them, by Braudel, saw the light of the day years after Kosambi's death. One may argue, as Thapar has done, that Kosambi could have read them in the original, given the fact that he had a good command over several European languages including French. But how do we know he didn't do that? Maybe he read them all and remained uninfluenced by them! Thapar may even charge Kosambi of being ignorant of the writings and ideas emanating from the Frankfurt School, which was gaining ground at the same time as the Annales and, in a similar vein, she may ridicule him for being unfamiliar with the writings of the Italian communist Antonio Gramsci (d.1937), who made significant departures from classical Marxism! Although similar captious criticisms can be multiplied to almost any length, a fair assessment of D.D. Kosambi should be made against the background of the thought currents which influenced him and not against those that passed him by. The finest Indian historians of today have remained uninfluenced by post-modernist thought, but does that minimize the importance of their contribution?

VIII

For all his rejection of some of the familiar formulations of Marx and Engels, Kosambi remained a Marxist and used their historical materialist method without showing a Procrustean adherence to it. He was unsparing in his denunciation of those who blindly repeated the conclusions of Marx and Engels all the time. His censorious verdict on S.A. Dange's *India from Primitive Communism to Slavery* (1949) is a case in point.[40]

Kosambi's history did not flourish 'under the aegis of the muse Clio who has an abacus to determine chronology' and 'a trumpet to celebrate the victories of kings and generals'. He rescued history from the chroniclers of 'personal', 'episodic' and drum-and-trumpet history of India, which 'should be enjoyed as a romantic fiction' or 'some Indian railway time table', and focused on the history of the people.[41] The more important question, according to him, is not who was king or whether a given region had a king, but whether its people used a plough, light or heavy, at the time. He thus highlighted the important role of technology and economic production, the productive forces which catalysed major social and political change. He spoke of the transforming role of iron in the context of the Ganga valley during the post-Vedic period, which saw the dispersal of agriculture, availability of economic surplus, growth of urban centres and the formation of states in the region. In one of her recent writings Romila Thapar concedes that the 'crucial questions in Kosambi's argument are still relevant', but she underplays the role of technology by arguing that the archaeological presence of iron at the Megalithic sites in peninsular India was not accompanied by the kind of developments seen in north India, and thus lends colour to the assertions of those who deny the role of technology, especially the use of iron in early north India. Admittedly, the study of social change through the prism of technological and economic developments is complex and gives rise to problems. For example, Kosambi's view that Buddhism declined in India with the decline of trade and the emergence of closed village economic units when the vast Buddhist monastic foundations became a drain on the economy is too simplistic to be convincing, especially when judged in the context of the Hindu temples. They acquired fabulous wealth through generous gifts and donations in the early medieval period, and used it for extending agriculture and augmenting agrarian production: but in course of time they became repositories of vast amounts of unproductive wealth and thus turned into a drain on the economy. If we go by Kosambi's explanation of Buddhism's decline, all famous Hindu temples should have decayed and dwindled from sheer neglect. However, Kosambi himself, being aware of the complexities in and limitations of the materialist approach, would not offer economic explanations for all historical developments. He therefore asserted that mere 'economic determinism will not do'[42] and that 'ideas (including superstition) become a force, once they have gripped the masses'.[43]

D.D. Kosambi's opposition to the colonial view of India as stagnant and having no history was vehement and forceful; and so was his antagonism to revivalism and obscurantism[44] as is borne out by some of his mordant and pungent statements about the popular religious dogmas and stereotypes. 'A modern orthodox Hindu,' he thus tells us, 'would place beef-eating on the same level as cannibalism, whereas Vedic Brahmins had fattened upon a steady diet of sacrificed beef.'[45] 'The Gita with its brilliant Sanskrit and superb inconsistency,' we are told, 'is a book that allows the reader to justify any action while shrugging off the consequences. The many-faceted god

[Krishna] is likewise inconsistent, though all things to all men and everything to most women.'[46] He also says of the *Gita:* 'This divine but rather scrambled message with its command of expository Sanskrit is characteristically Indian in attempting to reconcile the irreconcilable, in its power of gulping down sharp contradictions painlessly.'[47] And this is what he has to say about the much cherished notion of the 'golden age' of the Guptas, whom orthodox historians have credited with 'a revival of nationalism': 'Far from the Guptas reviving nationalism, it is nationalism that revived the Guptas'.[48] Such statements as these are unpalatable to the orthodox historians whose favourite pastimes has been to gild the lily at the cost of writing a serious history of the people. It would appear that the entire body of his research was intended to undermine the traditional bourgeois perception of the past, as is evident from the following:

The principal aim of history, as hitherto written, has been the presentation of great events in a chronological sequence. However, the relative importance of events rarely appears the same to the people of another time, place, civilisation, class bias, so that a mere chronicle does not suffice. The course of social development, the inner causes which ultimately manifest themselves in the striking events, the driving forces which underlie great movements, have to be made clear before any work can be dignified by the name of serious history. Yet this type of analysis is not always welcome to some historiographers. They, or the people who really condition their version of history, are unwilling to face the inevitable consequences of the procedure. For the implication is necessarily that all history can be so analysed, hence current events too; but if so, it follows that the course of events can be influenced by deliberate action, that history has hereafter to be consciously made by those that live it, not merely set down after a safe interval of time by the professional historian. This is clearly dangerous to those who would suffer by the change, usually those in power. Thus such historical writing is labelled subversive. History then remains a means of escape, a romantic pastime, a profession, or a method of inducing submissiveness; it cannot become a scientific pursuit.[49]

Kosambi's writings were subversive for both traditional historiography, and its patron, the Indian bourgeoisie. He succeeded in overthrowing the former insofar as much of the historical discourse veers round his ideas even several decades after his death. The Indian bourgeoisie, however, has gained in strength and is more prosperous now than it ever was. The paradigm shift in historiography has not been accompanied by a corresponding power shift in politics. The current power shift, with the rise of the Sangh Parivar, is only promoting obscurantism, hyper nationalism and fascism.

NOTES

1. Anindya Chatterjee, 'An Introduction to the Proper Orthogonal Decomposition', *Current Science*, vol. 78, no. 7, 10 April 2000, p. 808.
2. C.K. Raju, 'Kosambi the Mathematician', in D.N. Jha, ed., *The Many Careers of D.D. Kosambi*, Delhi, 2011.
3. 'Scientific Numismatics', *Scientific American* (February 1966), pp. 102-11. Between 1940 and 1966 he wrote no less than a dozen articles on punch-marked coins, the earliest coinage of India, which were published under the sponsorship of the Indian Council of Historical Research (ICHR), New Delhi, under the title *Indian Numismatics*, Delhi, 1981. Another collection of 51 articles (excluding the numismatic studies) called *Historical Diversities*

was submitted by me to the ICHR in 1978. While its fate remains unknown to me, a similar volume of Kosambi's papers was published by the Oxford University Press, Delhi, in 2002. In the present essay I refer to the books and journals where Kosambi's writings were originally published.

4. R.S. Sharma, 'Coins and Problems of Early Economic History', *Journal of the Numismatic Society of India*, XXXI (1969), pp. 1-8. The original version of this paper was presented at a seminar held at the Patna University in 1967.
5. D.D. Kosambi, 'Steps in Science', *Science and Progress: Prof. D.D. Kosambi Commemoration Volume*, Bombay, 1974.
6. Sheldon Pollock, 'Towards a Political Philology: D.D. Kosambi and Sanskrit', *Economic and Political Weekly* (hereafter *EPW*), 26 July 2008, p. 53.
7. Ibid., pp. 52-3.
8. Albrecht Wezler, 'Preface', *The Epigrams Attributed to Bhartrihari*, ed. D.D. Kosambi, Delhi, 2000, p. ix.
9. The *Subhashitaratnakosha* compiled by Vidyakara, ed. D.D. Kosambi and V.V. Gokhale, Cambridge, 1957, Introduction.
10. Kosambi, 'Steps in Science', op. cit., p. 200.
11. Pollock, op. cit., p. 54.
12. D.D. Kosambi, *Exasperating Essays*, Delhi, 1957, p. 70.
13. *Subhashitaratnakosha*, Introduction, pp. xlv-lvii.
14. The scholars who have applauded Kosambi for his work in the field of literary text criticism are also the ones who have fiercely contested his views on the class character of Sanskrit poetry. For example, Pollock (op. cit., p. 54) has drawn attention to a thirteenth century literary anthology which praises the Sanskrit poetry of a simple potter named Ghrona and that of a Candala named Divakara.
15. D.D. Kosambi, 'The Working Class in the Amarakosa', *Journal of Oriental Research*, XXIV (1954-5), pp. 57-9.
16. D.D. Kosambi, *Myth and Reality*, Bombay, 1962, p. 42.
17. Ibid., pp. 15, 32.
18. Kosambi's approach to the study of the classical Sanskrit literature reminds us of his Western contemporaries who were major influences on the English educated youth of our generation.

Among them mention may be made of Christopher Caudwell (*Illusion and Reality*, *Studies and Further Studies in a Dying Culture*, etc.), George Thompson (*Aeschylus and Athens* and *Marxism and Poetry*), and Arnold Hauser (*Social History of Art*) to name only a few.

19. For a prejudiced view of Kosambi's archaeology see Shereen Ratnagar, 'Kosambi's Archaeology', *EPW*, XLIII, 30 July 2008, pp. 71-7.
20. Ibid. p. 71.
21. *The Times of India*, 13 October 1964.
22. *An Introduction to the Study of Indian History* (hereafter *Introduction)*, Bombay, 1956, p. 5.
23. *Culture and Civilisation of Ancient India in Historical Outline* (hereafter *Culture)*, London, 1965, p. 13.
24. *Myth and Reality*, p. 2.
25. Kosambi expounded his research methodology in the following two articles: 'Combined Methods in Indology', *Indo-Iranian Journal*, vol. VI (1963), pp. 177-202; 'Living Prehistory in India', *Scientific American* (February 1967).
26. 'Combined Methods in Indology', *Indo-Iranian Journal*, VI.
27. *Culture,* p. 12.
28. *Introduction*, p. 10.
29. *Culture,* pp. 23-5.
30. Ibid., pp. 21-2.
31. Keith Hopkins, *Conquerors and Slaves*, Cambridge, 1978.
32. D.N. Jha, 'A Marxist View of Ancient Indian History', in Mohit Sen and M.B. Rao, eds., *Das Kapital Centenary Volume*, Delhi, 1967; idem, 'D.D. Kosambi', in S.P. Sen, ed., *Historians and Historiography in Modern India*, Calcutta, 1973, pp. 121-32.
33. Ibid.
34. R.S. Sharma, *Aspects of Political Ideas and Institutions in Ancient India*, 3rd edn., Delhi, 1991, chapter VI. For a detailed criticism of the application of the concept of Asiatic Mode of Production to the Indian situation see Brendan O'Leary, *The Asiatic Mode of Production*, London, 1989, chapter 7. The only Indian Marxist historian to have defended the concept and justified its application to India is Diptendra Banerjee. See his following two articles 'In

Search of a Theory of Pre-Capitalist Mode of Production' and 'Marx and the Original Form of India's Village Community', in Diptendra Banerjee, ed., *Marxian Theory and the Third World*, Delhi, 1985.

35. There is considerable ambiguity in Kosambi's position on the Asiatic Mode. In his *Introduction* (pp. 15-16, n. 14) he says: 'India showed a series of parallel forms which cannot be put into the precise categories. But in an article published in the *Journal of the Indo-Soviet Cultural Society* (vol. 1, 1954) he states that 'it is clear that an Asiatic mode did exist – at least the term is applicable to India, whatever the case elsewhere'. In a private conversation he told me that the editors of the journal had 'mutilated' his article beyond recognition.
36. Irfan Habib (*Seminar*, *Past and Present*, no. 39, 1962) and R.S. Sharma (*Journal of the Economic and Social History of the Orient*, 1958).
37. R.S. Sharma, *Indian Feudalism*, Calcutta, 1965.
38. In the context of European feudalism the Belgian historian Henri Pirenne, writing between the two Wars, argued that the classical world was founded on the unity of the Mediterranean Sea and the flourishing trade which this unity made possible. In the seventh century, however, the Arab followers of Muhammad disturbed this trade, as a result of which Europe was thrown back on its own agrarian resources. In the new situation where money revenues were absent, Charlemagne began the practice of supporting his soldiers through grants of land, thus creating the new feudal state and society and giving birth to the Middle Ages (*Economic and Social History of Medieval Europe*, London, 1936; *Mohammed and Charlemagne*, London, 1939).
39. Romila Thapar, *Interpreting Early India*, Delhi, 1992, pp. 110-11.
40. *Annals of the Bhandarkar Oriental Research Institute*, vol. 29 (1948), pp. 221-7.
41. According to a recent suggestion, Kosambi's emphasis on people's history was inspired by Rabindranath Tagore; though Leo Tolstoy had advocated as early as 1869 that 'historians should concern themselves not with heroes and battles but with the life of the people' in his *War and Peace*: see Eugenia Vanina, 'Some

Observations on Kosambi's Medieval India', in D.N. Jha, ed., *The Many Careers of D.D. Kosambi*, Delhi, 2011, p. 61.

42. *Culture,* p. 12.
43. *Introduction*, p. 10.
44. Although Kosambi did not write on medieval India (often described as 'Muslim' India by most historians), his attitude to the communal perception of the past can be gauged by his wry come back at R.C. Majumdar and K.M. Munshi who 'dismiss with contempt the nomenclature of the so-called Muslim Period'. He says: 'the proposal [to dismiss the Muslim period] is surpassingly incongruous when made by two Hindus with good Muslim professional names, Munshi and Majumdar'. See *Annals of the Bhandarkar Oriental Research Institute*, vol. 35 (1955), pp. 194-201.
45. *Culture,* p. 102.
46. Ibid., p. 114.
47. Ibid., p. 207.
48. *Introduction*, p. 313.
49. 'The Study of Ancient Indian Tradition', *Indica*, The Indian Historical Research Institute Silver Jubilee Commemoration Volume, Bombay, 1953.

NINE

Engaging with R.S. Sharma and his Historiography

BORN ON 1 SEPTEMBER 1920, Professor Ram Sharan Sharma (d. 20 August 2011) had his schooling in his village, Barauni, and at Begusarai, then a subdivisional town of Bihar. He joined Patna College in 1937 where he completed his Master's in history in 1943. After a brief stint at H.D. Jain College, Arrah and T.N.B. College, Bhagalpur, he became a lecturer in Patna College. In 1958 he took over as head of the Department of History, Patna University, which position he held until 1972 when he became the founder Chairman of the Indian Council of Historical Research (ICHR), New Delhi. In the following year he moved to the University of Delhi which offered him professorship and headship of its history department. At both Patna and Delhi he played a significant role in giving a radical direction to history teaching. Already at Patna University he had organized a national workshop in 1965 – perhaps the first of its kind in the country – to prepare a blueprint for the secularization, radicalization and decolonization of the history syllabi and had implemented many of his ideas there.[1] Soon after joining the University of Delhi in 1973, he convinced his colleagues in the Department of History and the undergraduate colleges, that curriculum revision, being linked with the ever increasing corpus of historical literature, should be a continuous process and create space for new interpretations of the past. With their support and cooperation he introduced drastic changes in the courses of study, and, inspired his successors who undertook similar exercise from time to time, often in the face of bitter opposition from the obscurantist and status quoist elements in the academic establishment and outside.

As an institution builder R.S. Sharma has few parallels. Both at Patna and Delhi universities he succeeded in expanding the history faculty by creating positions in new areas of historical research and making it academically active and vibrant. As the founder Chairman of the ICHR he created its infrastructure, initiated many projects which involved historians from different parts of the country and gave a truly national character to its activities. The projects relating to the publication of historical sources, translation of standard books and monographs in English into Indian languages, preparation of an epigraphic dictionary, historiographical surveys of the various areas of Indian history and the compilation of records on the national movement (known as the 'Towards Freedom' project as opposed to the 'Transfer of Power' by Nicholas Mansergh who viewed Indian freedom struggle from the British point of view), were all initiated during his chairmanship, and have, over the years, influenced research and teaching. The priority he accorded to the demystification of history and its reconstruction on secular and scientific lines, remained prominent in the ICHR's agenda before the Modi-led BJP captured power at the Centre. As an important member of the National Commission of the History of Sciences in India and of the UNESCO Commission on the History of Central Asian Civilizations he participated in the organization of the volumes published under their auspices. It was also largely because of his efforts that the largest body of professional Indian historians, the Indian History Congress, of which he was the General President in 1975, and which honoured him with H.K. Barpujari Award in 1987 and V.K. Rajwade National Award in 2002 for his life-long service and contribution to historical studies, has become the symbol of secular and scientific approach to history. In whatever capacity R.S. Sharma worked, his role bore the stamp of the academic vision and world-view he developed early in life.

In his youth R.S. Sharma, popularly known as R.S. among his friends and Sharmaji among his pupils, came in contact with several prominent personalities. One of them was the famous journalist, lawyer and social reformer, Sachidanand Sinha, the first president of the Constituent Assembly, in consultation with whom he prepared a report on the boundary dispute between Bihar and Bengal. But his association with Rahul Sankrityayan, the progressive polyglot and polymath who commanded respect of his contemporaries as well as the younger generation,

Karyanand Sharma, who began his political career with Non-Cooperation movement in 1920 and later emerged as an important leader of the peasant movement and the Communist Party of India, and with Swami Sahajanand Saraswati who founded the Bihar Provincial Kisan Sabha in 1929 and became the first president of the All India Kisan Sabha in 1936 had a much deeper influence on him. Sharmaji shared with them some of his personality traits like his spartan way of life, disarming humility and unpretentiousness, and an unstated, albeit perceptible, aversion to elitism, and, above all, his unquestionable personal and academic integrity which, throughout his professional career, presented a sharp contrast to those who plagiarize and prosper in the academic world.

With these qualities, Sharmaji could easily reach out to people from different walks of life; it was not an unusual sight to see him sitting on the Delhi University lawns and discussing with non-teaching staff their problems and, negotiating on their behalf in a situation of confrontation with the authorities. His simplicity and clarity of expression, reminiscent of Rahul Sankrityayan, was best reflected in his classroom lectures and in his writings which were all free of jargon; he never allowed his erudition to be overshadowed by obfuscation in the name of nuanced scholarship.

Through his association with persons like Rahul Sankrityayan and Karyanand Sharma as well as several freedom fighters he also enriched his own firsthand knowledge of the hard realities of rural life and its trials and tribulations and naturally moved to Marxist ideology and came close to the undivided Communist Party of India, whose leadership often sought his advice. Unlike the historians who turned to Marxism in the late 1950s and early 1960s only to disown it after gaining academic legitimacy, Prof. Sharma remained a Marxist throughout his life without drumbeating on Karl Marx. Far from being doctrinaire, his Marxism was pragmatic and pervades all his research work; there was nothing formulaic about his choice, and treatment of themes he wrote on. His aversion to the mechanical application of the ideas of Marx to the Indian situation is evident from his assessment of S.A. Dange's *India from Primitive Communism to Slavery* (1949) as more schematic than scholarly.

Prof. Sharma began his research career soon after he joined teaching. His early writings drew attention to the dharmashastric evidence which sought to equate women with property and shudras and highlighted their subservient position and exploitation; these anticipated the questioning, nearly four decades later, of A.S. Altekar's idealistic perception of women's status in ancient India which continues to remain influential, notwithstanding a plethora of research sponsored and inspired by the numerous feminist scholars, organizations and movements. He continued to express his interest in women's history from time to time,[2] but, in course of his professional career spanning over six decades, he focused his attention mainly on issues like caste and its inherent inequities, state formation and role of technology and its linkage with early Indian social formations, social context of ideology and so on, and produced *avant gardist* works on various aspects of Indian history.

II

British and Indian scholars before him had written about Indian social structure, especially the caste system; the former denounced the Indian society and the latter shied away from any discussion of its seamy side and adopted, by and large, a reformist approach. Some scholars influenced by Marxian ideas (e.g. A.N. Bose 1942-4; B.N. Dutt 1944; G.F. Ilyin 1952, S.A. Dange 1949, D.D. Kosambi 1946) also studied ancient Indian social structure and debunked many 'sedulously cherished myths of nationalist historiography' but did not pay attention to the travails of the lower orders which attracted the attention of B.R. Ambedkar (1946, 1948).[3] However, his flawed handling of the sources resulted in fallacious theories of the origin of shudras and untouchables. In a sense therefore R.S. Sharma was the first professional historian to make an in-depth analysis of sources stretching over a long period to trace the history of caste and delineate the vicissitudes of the lower social orders.

Sharma's path breaking work *Sudras in Ancient India*, a doctoral dissertation completed at the School of Oriental and African Studies, London, in 1956, was first published in 1958 and has had several editions ever since. Based on a rigorous scrutiny of a wide range of ancient Indian literary texts representing the brahminical world-view, it examined the position of the shudras and untouchables up to the end of the Gupta period, captured the voices of the oppressed masses in them and anticipated the later subaltern historiography, though, of course, without sharing the anti-Marxism of its enthusiastic exponents.

In his study of early Indian society, the main assumption of Sharma, unlike that of the British and other Western social scientists, notably Louis Dumont, was that it was not static but ever changing. He asserted that the position of the lower orders, inextricably linked with their changing relations with the means of production, underwent changes over time. This view, however, may not be acceptable to scholars, who, being averse to materialist explanation of historical phenomena, assign centrality to ritual hierarchy or to ritual purity/pollution in the formation and functioning of caste. Sharma's views on slavery, like those on the shudras and other lower sections, also may not be acceptable to many. The number of slaves in the Vedic period, he rightly suggests, was not large and, they worked mostly as domestic servants, having nothing to do with productive activities. When their number grew in the age of the Buddha, and in the Maurya period, slavery, according to him, '*played a very considerable role in agricultural production*' (emphasis added) but Sharma hesitates in describing the Mauryan society as 'slave society' and calls it a 'slave-owning society'[4] instead. Similarly, Sharma adduces evidence to show that in post-Maurya and Gupta times the social fabric was supported mainly by the tax paying vaishyas and the toiling shudras and describes it as 'vaishya-shudra society'[5] or 'vaishya-shudra social formation'.[6] These descriptive categories certainly indicate the changing nature of the early Indian social structure. But, being at variance with Marx's nomenclature of modes of production, they may also imply the incomparability of Indian caste system with non-

Indian societies and may be at odds with the universalism inherent in his Marxist method.

R.S. Sharma retained his interest in the study of ancient Indian social structure and its material basis throughout his professional career.[7] He produced original and insightful writings on social change and was the first to show that the early medieval period witnessed the proliferation of castes including the untouchable ones. But, puzzling though it may seem, he did not explain why the phenomena of caste and untouchability developed only in India and not elsewhere.

III

Connected with studies of social structure was Prof. R.S. Sharma's lasting interest in the formation and nature of early Indian state, and its social and economic underpinnings. He wrote many articles on Indian polity, and integrated the early ones in his *Aspects of Political Ideas and Institutions in Ancient India,* first published in 1959, and reprinted several times subsequently.[8] In this pioneering work, he broke away from traditional historiography in many ways. Thus unlike the nationalist historians who glorified early Indian state as a welfare state, equated it with the British constitutional monarchy, and postulated the existence of republics in ancient India, Sharma demonstrated the caste/class dimension of state, exposed its exploitative character and argued that the so-called 'republics' were tribal oligarchies or at best 'distorted' republics.[9] Unlike his predecessors and contemporaries, he identified the stages in the development of ancient

Indian polity and, drew attention to the distinctive features of the administrative systems under the Mauryas, Satavahanas, Kushanas, Guptas and later dynasties, though his endorsement of and emphasis on the traditional perception of the Maurya state as centralized may not go well with some scholars. But he offered a well argued analysis of the various dimensions of the complex origin of early Indian state and its various phases in his *Origin of the State in India* (1989) and *The State and Varna Formation in the Mid-Ganga Plains: An Ethnoarchaeological View* (1996). Sharma's keenness to identify elements of change led him to question even the tenability of the Marxian concept of Asiatic/Oriental despotism subsuming a static state and society, an exercise undertaken by several scholars before and after him.[10] R.S. Sharma was also critical of his contemporaries whose excessive use of sociological verbiage, often ignored the material basis of major social transformation; his magisterial critique of the much talked about model of segmentary state is an example of his engagement with them.[11]

IV

Averse to exaggerating the role of ritual, religion and tradition in ancient Indian social polity and wary of using fashionable and woolly anthropological concepts as analytical tools,[12] Sharma examined the various aspects of early Indian social formation including the emergence of state from a materialist point of view. He published quite a few articles from the late 1960s onward which analysed the transition from Vedic pastoralism to post-

Vedic sedentary agriculture and consequent unleashing of the processes of surplus production, urbanization, consolidation of caste system and the rise of a tax paying class, state formation, and the emergence of heterodoxies (Jainism and Buddhism). Like D.D. Kosambi, he argued that iron technology played a catalytic role in this major social transformation – a view endorsed by many scholars including Romila Thapar (if only to dilute her position subsequently!)[13] – and criticized by others like A. Ghosh and Nihar Ranjan Ray.[14] Although Sharma reacted to his critics from time to time,[15] he provided a comprehensive response to them in his seminal work *Material Culture and Social Formations in Ancient India* (1983, chapters I and VI). Here, far from treating iron technology as the sole factor of social change, he viewed it as part of the general growth of productive forces which paved the way for a sedentary agricultural society in later Vedic and post-Vedic times. Like Gordon Childe, he believed that the evolution and functioning of technology can be best understood in its social context and that no linear cause-and-effect relationship between it and social change can be postulated.[16]

V

R.S. Sharma is always associated with the study of feudalism in early India. Both before and after him several historians mentioned feudalism in their own way[17] but he was the first to undertake its comprehensive study by publishing an article in 1958 and then a full-length book *Indian Feudalism* in 1965.[18] In these writings, he basically argued (i) that feudalism in India, unlike in Europe, was causally linked with the practice of making land grants to brahmins, temples and monasteries which began from the first century BC and became widespread from the middle of the first millennium onwards; and, (ii) that, despite different origins, the economic essence of the feudal phenomena in both the regions lay in the emergence of landed intermediaries leading to the enserfment of peasantry through restrictions on its mobility and freedom, increasing obligation to perform forced labour (*vishti*), mounting tax burdens and the evils of subinfeudation. The crucial element in Sharma's chain of arguments was the premise that there took place around the middle of the first millennium AD, a decline in commodity production, urban centres and foreign trade resulting in the growth of a self-sufficient economy in which metallic currency became relatively scarce and hence all payments (whether to priests or to the government officials) had to be made through assignment of land or land revenue.[19]

Arguments of Sharma, based on empirically valid premises formulated by him in his early writings on feudalism sound neat and logical, but seem theoretically inadequate; for they seek to explain feudal developments solely in terms of foreign trade which declined, to a large extent, due to factors external to the Indian situation. Like Kosambi, he overemphasizes the importance of foreign trade and seems to deny any built-in potential for change in the early Indian society – a position implicit in the concept of Asiatic Mode of Production which is unacceptable to him. Thus the rejection of the concept of the Asiatic Mode of Production (1975) on the one hand and acceptance of the idea of feudal transformation caused by factors not directly related to the Indian context on the other gave rise to a theoretical impasse. This led to a rethinking on the part of Prof. Sharma and, in a paper presented at the annual session of the Indian History Congress at Hyderabad in 1978,[20] he argued, for the first time, that the Indian society itself was passing through a phase of crisis in the early centuries AD. He drew attention to the third-fourth century epic and Puranic descriptions of the Kali age which indicate a deep social and economic turmoil. He had in fact referred to Kali age in his book on the shudras as early as 1958 but now, on the basis of a detailed analysis, he asserted that it was a phase of sharp social conflict leading to the weakening of the traditional brahminical social order and to the development of a new mechanism of surplus extraction and its redistribution. This basically meant that the state now gave up the earlier practice of collecting taxes through its agents and then remunerating its employees; it now began to assign land and land revenues directly to the priests, military officers and other employees as their remuneration. The significance of this theory lies in the fact that, without contradicting the earlier explanation of transition to feudalism in terms of external factors like decline of trade, it tries to locate the genesis of feudal formation in internal social dynamics.

Many inscriptions from different parts of the country also refer to Kali age crisis, the earliest being a second century Satavahana record. But doubts may still be raised about the validity of any historical explanation based on it. The Kali age is described in most of the Puranic texts, and even if we keep the medieval Puranas out of consideration, it is possible to identify at least three sets of its descriptions assignable to the third-fourth, eighth and tenth centuries. Since most of these descriptions are conventional and repetitive, their chronology as well as their value for historical reconstruction becomes uncertain. Also, it is intriguing that although the epic and Puranic passages which describe the Kali age and are cited by Sharma to buttress his argument do not mention the *kalivarjyas* (practices forbidden in the *kaliyuga*), which seem to have begun to be mentioned in the texts around the end of the first millennium or the beginning of the second; Apararka (1125) was among the earliest to refer to them. But the *kalivarjyas* were finally codified not earlier than the seventeenth century by Damodara in his *Kalivarjyavinirnaya*. Thus instead of dismissing the Kali explanation *tout court,* it is necessary to subject the relevant literary and epigraphical material to a rigorous examination.

The applicability of the European feudal model to the early medieval agrarian situation also remains problematic as was pointed out as early as 1979.[21] For example, the manorial system which is often treated as a characteristic feature of European feudalism was absent in India; and it may be difficult to equate European serfdom with the forms of bondage of Indian peasantry. Sharma at some stage conceded the first point but continued to maintain that serfs/semi-serfs played a crucial role in agricultural production in India much as they did in medieval Europe. In other words, serfdom, in his view, was a salient feature of both European and early medieval Indian agrarian society. But this view has also come in for much criticism and debate has often centred round the meaning, nature and scope of serfdom.[22] However, without going into the semantic history of the word, serfdom, if used in the Indian context, may be understood in the sense of generalized servility of peasants. For there is little doubt that, notwithstanding the enthusiastic advocacy of a free peasantry in India,[23] the ordinary peasants in the early medieval period and later have been servile. Peasant rebellions discussed by Sharma (1988) and M.G.S. Narayanan (1988) provide ample evidence of the unfreedom of peasants;[24] their contradiction with landed intermediaries, is supported by medieval and modern instances of peasant resistance, the more recent ones being the anti-zamindari unrest in Bihar (1930s), Tebhaga movement in Bengal (1946), and Telangana rebellion in Andhra Pradesh (1946-51).

Criticism of Sharma's Eurocentric approach may have some substance, but it is necessary to bear in mind that a historian adopting a universalistic approach to the study of the past may find it difficult to jettison the comparative method, even if comparisons may not always be valid. Also, Eurocentrism, like Orientalism, has a history. It is rooted in the academic tradition in which several generations of historians including that of Professor Sharma grew up, so that if one were to adopt a comparative approach to India's past, European parallels would come in handy, though this should not preclude the comparison of Indian historical developments with those in other Asian or non-European countries.

Sharma's work on 'Indian feudalism', despite all

reservations, represents the dominant perception of early medieval Indian social formation, including the feudal mentality and the material context of religious ideologies.[25] It was a landmark in Indian historiography, and has been debated widely among historians and other social scientists. It has received acclaim as well as adverse appraisals. Some of Sharma's critics have, however, displayed an extraordinary enthusiasm in questioning the premises on which Sharma's feudal model is founded. Thus one of them, while arguing against the idea of urban decay, has asserted, on the basis of inscriptional references, that several urban centres like Prithudaka (Pehoa), Tattanandapura (Ahar), Siyadoni (near Jhansi) and Gopagiri (Gwalior) flourished with extensive market networks during the early medieval period.[26] But the crucial epigraphic evidence, on which the above observation is based, relates to the ninth-tenth century and does not contradict the contention of Sharma; on the contrary it is in line with his view that the centuries immediately preceding the Turkish conquest witnessed a revival of trade and towns.[27] Similarly his notion of the relative paucity of coins during the fifth-tenth-century period, linked with decline of trade and towns, has been called into question on the basis of either later or slender evidence.[28] Despite criticisms Sharma's assertions about de-urbanization and currency contraction are unassailable; for they are amply supported by a mélange of archaeological and numismatic data presented in his *Urban Decay in India c. 300-1000* (1987) and the Nathaniel Wallich Memorial Lecture at Indian Museum, Calcutta (1988), incorporated in his *Early Medieval Indian Society* (2001, chapter 4).[29]

VI

Scholars may not agree with specific statements or general conclusions of Prof. Sharma but there is no denying the fact that the entire corpus of his research had an anti-communal dimension and had much bearing on the periodization of Indian history. Communal historiography based on James Mill's division of India's precolonial history into 'Hindu' and 'Muslim' periods, adopted and popularized by Vincent Smith (1904), assigns a fantastic antiquity, imagined purity, and irrational indigenist origin to the Hindu culture which reached its high watermark during the so-called 'golden age of the Guptas'. But Prof. Sharma was consistently opposed to this perception of pre-Islamic traits of Indian history. At a time when the high priests of communal historiography, K.M. Munshi and R.C. Majumdar, adopting Mill's periodization, glorified the 'Hindu period' as one of great achievements and denounced the 'Muslim period' as one of decline and degradation, Sharma was perhaps the first to do away with the Hindu-Muslim binary and to write about the depressed position of the shudras, feudal exploitation, and social tension at various levels. Therefore in 1977, when the Janata Party came to power, the communalist and obscurantist forces were up in arms against the NCERT textbooks written by secular historians like R.S. Sharma, and launched a vicious attack on his *Ancient India* and succeeded in getting it banned. But he mobilized the support of his colleagues and other history teachers along with many social scientists throughout the country in favour of his book and wrote a booklet *In Defence of Ancient India* (1978). The demand for the restoration of his book took the form of a popular movement of academics in the country and consequently the ban was withdrawn.

Prof. Sharma displayed a remarkable foresight in his fight against communalism so that even before the rabidly communal Ramjanmabhoomi movement gained momentum, he moved the Indian History Congress to pass the resolution year after year for the protection of the Baburi Masjid. He himself, along with his three other colleagues and friends, participated as independent scholars in the parleys between the protagonists of the Temple movement and the members of the Baburi Masjid Action Committee. He also wrote extensively in the newspapers and magazines and exposed the communalist attempt to distort the history of Ayodhya. He published a booklet *Communal History and Rama's Ayodhya* (1990) and, authored, jointly with three scholars, *Ramjanamabhumi-Baburi Masjid: A Historians' Report to the Nation* (1991) focusing on the historical issues involved in the Ayodhya imbroglio. He was thus in the forefront of secular academics combating the communal elements and provided them with an ideological weapon through his writings which, were an antidote to communalist onslaught culminating in the demolition of the mosque – a dastardly act which the World Archaeology Congress III (1994) condemned in the strongest terms at the initiative of Prof. Sharma, despite vehement opposition from the Indian archaeological establishment which has been a citadel of communalism and revivalism. Prof. Sharma's crusade against Hindu communalists and xenophobes continued unabated even later and his two books – *Looking for the Aryans* (1995) and *Advent of the Aryans in India* (1999), written in the best tradition of historical scholarship, convincingly refute the propaganda of the Aryan autochthony. He fought against communalism and xenophobia all his life and did all that he could for maintaining the country's secular social fabric.

VII

The importance of the research of Prof. Sharma lies not only in the fact that he broke new grounds in the field of early Indian history but also in his critical approach to the sources. Historians before him used inscriptions for writing dynastic history and for fixing the chronology of kings and their battles, but he asked new questions of them and used them for reconstructing the social, economic and cultural history of India.[30] Unlike the Indologists who used coins for working out the minor details of political history and finding out their specific metal content, he fruitfully used them for writing monetary history and for determining the level of monetization of early Indian economy at a particular point of time.[31] Unlike the Indian archaeologists, who used artefacts and antiquities for satisfying their insatiable antiquarian appetite, he used them as a source for the history of early Indian settlements and urban centres.[32] His mastery over different types of sources coupled with his understanding of the current anthropological and sociological theories gave Sharma an edge over most of his peers. He gave the slogan '*no theory, no history*' but he did not build theories in the air. He broke the stereotype of a stagnant and ahistoric Indian society trumpeted by Western scholars just as he exploded the myth of a glorious 'Hindu' India orchestrated by Indian historians, thus making sharp departures from both colonial and nationalist historiographies. He shifted the focus of history writing from the annals of kings and queens to the narration of the travails of the underprivileged and the marginalized people, took Indian history away from the realm of myths and legends and demystified it. He fought for a scientific history of the Indian people and spurned those who merely romanticized the past and gilded the lily. Prof. R.S. Sharma's oeuvre remains a welcome contrast to the fashionable studies in which 'social criticism floats free of any universalist theoretical ground' and provides an antidote to the writings of the avowedly anti-Marxist new thinkers who sing 'the virtues of the empire', and seem to extend a warm welcome to 'a new world order dominated by imperial warlords, corporate profiteers and neo-liberal ideologues'.

NOTES

1. 'Problems of Research in History in Indian Universities', *Quarterly Review of Historical Studies,* 1, no. 2, 1963; 'The Organisation of Historical Research in Indian Universities', *Quarterly Review of Historical Studies,* III, 1963-4, pp. 127-9. 'Some General Suggestions, Undergraduate Teaching in History', *Proceedings of Seminar on Undergraduate Teaching of History,* Patna, 1968, pp. 6-11.
2. 'Traces of Promiscuity in Ancient Indian Society', *Proceedings of the Indian History Congress,* 19th Session, Agra, 1956, pp. 153-7; 'Problems of Social Formation in Early India', General President's Address, *Proceedings of the Indian History Congress,* 36th Session,

Aligarh, 1975, pp. 1-14; 'Historical Aspects of Sati', *Social Science Probings*, vol. 6, nos. 1-4, January-December 1989.

3. *Who Were the Shudras?*, Bombay, 1946; *The Untouchables*, Delhi, 1948.
4. *Sudras in Ancient India: A Social History of the Lower Order Down to circa AD 600*, Delhi, 1958, 3rd rev. edn. 1990, rpt. 2002, p. 183.
5. Ibid., p. 322.
6. Ibid., p. 260.
7. E.g. *Social Changes in Early Medieval India*, First Devaraj Chanana Memorial Lecture, Delhi, 1969; 'Problems of Social Formation in Early India', General President's Address, *Proceedings Indian History Congress*, Aligarh, 1975, pp. 1-14; 'Class Formation and its Material Basis in the Upper Gangetic Basin (*c.* 1000-500 BC)', *The Indian Historical Review*, vol. II, no.1, July 1975, 1-13.
8. *Aspects of Political Ideas and Institutions in Ancient India*, Delhi, 1959, 5th revd. edn., 2005.
9. Ibid., p. 132.
10. R.S. Sharma, 'The Socio-Economic Bases of Oriental Despotism in Early India', in S.K. Bose (ed.), *Essays in Honour of Dr Gyanchand*, Delhi, 1981. D.D. Kosambi, 'The Basis of Despotism', *The Economic Weekly*, 2 November 1957, pp. 1417-19; Irfan Habib, 'An Examination of Wittfogel's Theory of Oriental Despotism,' *Enquiry*, no. 6 (Old Series), 1962; Bipan Chandra, 'Karl Marx, His Theories of Asian Societies and Colonial Rule', *Review*, vol. V, no. 1 (Summer 1981); Brendan O'Leary, *The Asiatic Mode of Production: Oriental Despotism, Historical Materialism and Indian History*, Oxford, 1989.
11. 'The Segmentary State and the Indian Experience', *Indian Historical Review*, vol. XVI, nos. 1-2, July 1989-January 1990, pp. 90-108.
12. R.S. Sharma, 'From Kin to Class' [being a review of Romila Thapar's *From Lineage to State*], *Economic and Political Weekly*, vol. XX, no. 22 (1 June 1985), pp. 960-1. For Sharma's detailed comments on anthropological approach see his *Material Culture and Social Formations in Ancient India*, Delhi, 1983, chapter I.
13. Sharma made a clear reference to the significant role of iron technology in the process of social change in 1968: Material

Background of the Origin of Buddhism', in Mohit Sen (ed.), *Das Kapital Centenary Volume*, Delhi, 1968, pp. 59-66. The following year, in her address to the Indian History Congress (Ancient India section), Romila Thapar, echoed 'comparable' sentiments about the impact of the new technology on people's lives but which, a scholar strangely enough informs us, 'was wrongly construed and misunderstood': B.P. Sahu (ed.), *Iron and Social Change in Early India*, Delhi, 2006, Introduction, pp. 4-5.

14. A. Ghosh, *The City in Early Historical India*, Simla, 1973, pp. 5-15, 90; Nihar Ranjan Ray, 'Technology and Social Change in Early Indian History', *Puratattva*, no. 8 (1975-6), pp. 132-8.
15. 'Iron and Urbanisation in the Ganga Basin', *The Indian Historical Review*, vol. I, no. 1, March 1974, pp. 98-103.
16. There is nothing new about controversy centring round the role of technology in history. In the late 1930s and early 1940s, Gordon Childe wrote his most popular works highlighting the role of technology and never met the approval of the British archaeological establishment; in the early 1950s Needham began to publish his volumes on science and civilization in China and his critics charged him of exaggerating her technological achievements; in early 1960s Lynn White Jr wrote on medieval technology and social change and he was faulted for linking it with medieval Christianity; a few years later, in 1969, Irfan Habib delivered his presidential address on medieval technology at the Indian History Congress and he was criticized for assigning the introduction of the Persian wheel in India to the period of the Turkish conquests and the centuries that immediately followed them. All this, however, does not minimize the significant role of technology in social change. Criticism of 'technicism' comes, not infrequently, from its beneficiaries!
17. Bhupendra Nath Datta, *Studies in Indian Social Polity*, Calcutta, 1944; idem, *Dialectics of Land Economics of India*, Calcutta, 1952; Nihar Ranjan Ray, *Bangalir Itihas*, Calcutta, 1949; idem, *The Medieval Factor in Indian History*, General President's Address, Indian History Congress, Patiala, 1967; D.D. Kosambi, 'Origin of Feudalism in Kashmir', *Journal of Bombay Branch of the Royal Asiatic Society*, vols. 31-2 (1956-7); idem, *Introduction to the Study*

of Indian History, Bombay, 1956; Lallanji Gopal, 'On Some Problems of Feudalism in Ancient India', *Annals of the Bhandarkar Oriental Institute*, vol. XLIV (1963); *The Economic Life of Northern India (c. AD 700-1200)*, Delhi, 1965.

18. 'The Origins of Feudalism in India (*c.* AD 400-650)', *Journal of the Economic and Social History of the Orient*, vol. 1, no. 3 (October 1958), pp. 297-328; *Indian Feudalism: c. 300-1200*, Calcutta, 1965.
19. *Indian Feudalism,* chapter I.
20. The paper was later published as 'The Kali Age: A Period of Social Crisis', in S.N. Mukherjee (ed.), *Indian History and Thought: Essays in Honour of A.L. Basham,* Calcutta, 1982.
21. D.N. Jha, 'Early Indian Feudalism: A Historiographical Critique', Presidential Address, Indian History Congrees, Waltair, 1979; idem, *The Feudal Order*, Delhi, 2000, Editor's Introduction.
22. Vishwa Mohan Jha, *Serfdom as a Category of Historical Analysis*, R.K. Chowdhry Memorial Lecture, Darbhanga, 2011.
23. Harbans Mukhia, 'Was there Feudalism in Indian History', Presidential Address (Medieval India section), Indian History Congress, Waltair, 1979. For a response from R.S. Sharma see his 'How Feudal was Indian Feudalism?', *The Journal of Peasant Studies*, XII, nos. 2 & 3, January/April 1985, pp. 19-43. Also see idem, 'Urbanism and the Use of Metal Money in Early India', 12th Conference of International Association of Historians of Asia, University of Hong-Kong, June 1991.
24. 'Problems of Peasant Protests in Early Medieval India', *Social Scientist,* vol. 16, no. 9 (September 1988), also see *Economic History of Early India,* Delhi, 2011; M.G.S. Narayanan, 'The Role of Peasants in the Early History of Tamilkam in South India', *Social Scientist*, vol. 16, no. 9 (September 1988).
25. 'An Approach to Archaeology and Divination in Mediaeval India', in Horst Krüger (ed.), *Neue Indienkunde New Indology: Festschrift Walter Ruben zun 70. Geburstg*, Berlin, 1970; 'Economic and Social Basis of Tantrism' and 'The Feudal Mind' in his *Early Medieval Indian Society: A Study in Feudalisation* (Hyderabad, 2001).
26. B.D. Chattopadhyaya, 'Trade and Urban Centres in Early Medieval North India', *Indian Historical Review*, vol. 1, no. 2 (1974); idem, 'Urban Centres in Early Medieval India: An

Overview', in S. Bhattacharya and Romila Thapar (eds.), *Situating Indian History: For Sarvapalli Gopal,* Delhi, 1986.

27. *Indian Feudalism*, chapter VI.
28. For further discussion see D.N. Jha (ed.), *The Feudal Order,* Editor's Introduction, pp. 4-6.
29. For a convincing response to criticisms of Sharma's feudal model and allied issues see Krishna Mohan Shrimali, 'Reflections on Recent Perceptions of Early Medieval India', Presidential Address (Historiography Section), Andhra Pradesh History Congress, Tenali, 1994.
30. R.S. Sharma, 'Land Grants and Early Indian Economic History', in his *Light on Early Indian Society and Economy,* Bombay, 1966.
31. R.S. Sharma, 'Coins and Problems of Early Economic History', in his *Perspectives in Social and Economic History of Early India,* Delhi, 1983; idem, *Early Medieval Indian Society: A Study in Feudalisation*.
32. R.S. Sharma, 'Decay of Gangetic Towns in Gupta and Post-Gupta Times', *Proceedings of the Indian History Congress,* 33rd Session, Muzaffarpur, 1972, pp. 94-105; idem, *Urban Decay in India c. 300-1000*, Delhi, 1987.

TEN

Responding to a Communalist*

I WAS AMUSED to read 'How History was Made up at Nalanda' (*Indian Express*, 28 June 2014), by Arun Shourie who has dished out to readers his ignorance masquerading as knowledge – reason enough to have pity on him and sympathy for his readers! Since he has referred to me by name and has charged me with fudging evidence to distort the historical narrative of the destruction of the ancient Nalandamahavihar, I consider it necessary to rebut his allegations and set the record straight instead of ignoring his balderdash.

My presentation at the Indian History Congress in 2006 (and not 2004 as stated by Shourie), to which he refers, was not devoted to the destruction of ancient Nalanda per se – his account misleads readers and pulls wool over their eyes. It was in fact focused on the antagonism between the brahmins and Buddhists for which I drew on different kinds of evidence including myths and traditions. In this context I cited the tradition

*This response to Arun Shourie was carried by the Kafila website on 9 July 2014. Its shorter version was published in *The Indian Express* the same day as 'How History was Unmade at Nalanda'.

recorded in the eighteenth century Tibetan text, *Pag-sam-jon-zang* by Sumpa Khan-Po Yece Pal Jor, mentioned by B.N.S. Yadava in his *Society and Culture in Northern India in the Twelfth Century* (p. 346) with due acknowledgement, though in his pettiness, Shourie is quick to discover plagiarism on my part! I may add that 'Hindu fanatics' are not my words but Yadav's which is why they are in quotes. How sad that one has to point this out to a Magsaysay awardee journalist!

In his conceit Shourie is disdainful and dismissive of the Tibetan tradition which, has certain elements of miracle in it, as recorded in the text. Here is the relevant extract from Sumpa's work cited by Shourie: 'While a religious sermon was being delivered in the temple that he [Kakut Siddha] had erected at Nalanda, a few young monks threw washing water at two Tirthika beggars. (The Buddhists used to designate the Hindus by the term Tirthika.) The beggars being angry, set fire on the three shrines of Dharmaganja, the Buddhist University of Nalanda, viz. – Ratna Sagara, Ratna Ranjaka including the nine-storeyed temple called Ratnodadhi which contained the library of sacred books' (p. 92). Shourie questions how the two beggars could go from building to building to 'burn down the entire, huge, scattered complex'. Look at another passage (abridged by me in the following paragraph) from the *History of Buddhism in India* written by another Tibetan monk and scholar Taranatha in the seventeenth century:

During the consecration of the temple built by Kakutsiddha at Nalendra [Nalanda] 'the young naughty sramanas threw slops at the two tirthika beggars and kept them pressed inside door panels and set ferocious dogs on them'. Angered by this, one of them went on arranging for their livelihood and the other sat in a deep pit and 'engaged himself in *surya sadhana*' [solar worship], first for nine years and then for three more years and having thus 'acquired mantrasiddhi' he 'performed a sacrifice and scattered the charmed ashes all around' which 'immediately resulted in a miraculously produced fire', consuming all the eighty four temples and the scriptures some of which, however, were saved by water flowing from an upper floor of the nine storey Ratnodadhi temple (*History of Buddhism in India,* English tr. Lama Chimpa and Alka Chattopadhyaya, summary of pp. 141-2).

If we look at the two narratives closely, they are similar. The role of the Tirthikas and their miraculous fire causing a conflagration are common to both. Admittedly one does not have to take the miracles literally but it is not justified to ignore their importance as part of traditions which gain in strength over time and become part of collective memory of the community. Nor is it desirable or defensible to disregard the element of long standing antagonism between the brahmins and Buddhists which may have given rise to the Tibetan tradition and nurtured it till as late as the eighteenth century or even later. It is in the context of this Buddhist-Tirthika animosity that the account of Sumpa assumes importance; it also makes sense because it fits in with Taranatha's evidence. Further, neither Sumpa, nor Taranatha, ever came to India. This should mean that the idea of brahminical hostility to the religion of the Buddha travelled to Tibet fairly early and became part of its Buddhist tradition, and found expression in the seventeenth-eighteenth century Tibetan writings. Acceptance or rejection of this kind of source-criticism is welcome if it comes from a professional historian and but not from someone who flirts with history as Shourie does.

Of the two Tibetan traditions, the one referred to by me has been given credence not only by Yadava (whom Shourie, in his ignorance, dubs a Marxist!) but a number of other Indian scholars like R.K. Mookerji (*Education in Ancient India*), Sukumar Dutt (*Buddhist Monks and Monsteries of India*), Buddha Prakash (*Aspects of Indian History and Civilization*), and S.C. Vidyabhushana who interprets the text to say that it refers to an actual 'scuffle between the Buddhist and brahminical mendicants and the latter, being infuriated, propitiated the Sun god for twelve years, performed a fire-sacrifice and threw the living embers and ashes from the sacrificial pit into the Buddhist temples which eventually destroyed the great library at Nalanda called Ratnodadhi' (*History of Indian Logic*, p. 516 as cited by D.R. Patil, *The Antiquarian Remains in Bihar*, p. 327). Scholars named above were all polymaths of unimpeachable academic honesty and integrity. They had nothing to do, even remotely, with Marxism, which is a red rag to Shourie in his bull *avatar*.

Now juxtapose the Tibetan tradition with the contemporary account in the *Tabaqat-i-Nasiri* of Minhaj-i-Siraj, which Shourie not only misinterprets but also blows out of proportion. Although its testimony has no bearing on my argument about brahminical intolerance, a word needs to be said about it so as to expose his 'false knowledge', which as G.B. Shaw said, is 'more dangerous than ignorance'. The famous passage from this text reads *exactly* as follows:

He [Bakhtiyar Khalji] used to carry his depredations into those parts and that country until he organized an attack upon the fortified city of Bihar. Trustworthy persons have related on this wise, that he advanced to the gateway of the fortress of Bihar with two hundred horsemen in defensive armour, and suddenly attacked the place. There were two brothers of Farghanah, men of learning, one Nizamu-ud-Din, the other Samsam-ud-Din (by name) in the service of Muhammad-i-Bakht-yar; and the author of this book [Minhaj] met with at Lakhnawati in the year 641 H., and this account is from him. These two wise brothers were soldiers among that band of holy warriors when they reached the gateway of the fortress and began the attack, at which time Muhammad-i-Bakhtiyar, by the force of his intrepidity, threw himself into the postern of the gateway of the place, and they captured the fortress and acquired great booty. The greater number of inhabitants of that place were Brahmans, and the whole of those Brahmans had their heads shaven; and they were all slain. There were a great number of books there; and, when all these books came under the observation of the Musalmans, they summoned a number of Hindus that they might give them information respecting the import of those books; but the whole of the Hindus were killed. On becoming acquainted (with the contents of the books), it was found that the whole of that fortress and city was a college, and in the Hindui tongue, they call a college Bihar. (*Tabaqat-i-Nasiri*, English tr. H.G. Raverty, pp. 551-2)

The above account mentions the fortress of Bihar as the target of Bakhtiyar's attack. The fortified monastery which Bakhtiyar captured was, 'known as Audand-Bihar or Odandapura-vihara' (Odantapuri in Biharsharif then known simply as Bihar). This is the view of many historians but, most importantly, of Jadunath Sarkar, the high priest of communal historiography in India (*History of Bengal*, vol. 2, pp. 3-4). Minhaj does not refer to Nalanda at all: he merely speaks of the ransacking of the 'fortress of Bihar' (hisar-i-Bihar). But how can Shourie be satisfied unless Bakhtiyar is shown to have sacked Nalanda? Since Bakhtiyar was leading plundering expeditions in the region of Magadha, Shourie thinks that Nalanda must have been destroyed by him – and, magically, he finds 'evidence' in an account which does not even speak of the place. Thus an important historical testimony becomes the victim of his anti-Muslim prejudice. In his zeal, he fudges and concocts historical evidence and ignores the fact that Bakhtiyar did not go to Nalanda; it 'escaped the main fury of the Muslim conquest because it lay not on the main route from Delhi to Bengal but needed a separate expedition' (A.S. Altekar in his Introduction to Roerich's *Biography of Dharmasvamin*). Also, a few years after Bakhtiyar's sack of Odantapuri, when the Tibetan monk Dharmasvamin visited Nalanda in 1234, he 'found some buildings unscathed' in which some pandits and monks resided and received instruction from Mahapandita Rahulshribhadra. In fact, Bakhtiyar seems to have proceeded from Biharshrif to Nadia in Bengal through the hills and jungles of the region of Jharkhand, which, incidentally, finds first mention in an inscription of 1295 AD (*Comprehensive History of India*, vol. IV, pt. I, p. 601).

I may add that his whole book, *Eminent Historians*, from which the article under reference is excerpted, abounds in instances of cavalier attitude to historical evidence and peddles a perverse perception of the Indian past.

It is neither possible nor necessary to deny that the Islamic invaders conquered parts of Bihar and Bengal and destroyed the famous universities in the region. But Shourie's laboured effort to associate Bakhtiyar Khalji with the destruction and burning of the university of Nalanda is a glaring example of the wilful distortion of history. Certainly weekend historians like Shourie and others of his tribe are always free to falsify historical data but this only reveals the lack of any serious historical training.

Shourie had raised a huge controversy by publishing his scandalous and slanderous *Eminent Historians* in 1998 during the NDA regime and now, after sixteen years, he has issued its second edition. He appears and reappears in the historian's *avatar* when the BJP comes to power, tries to please his masters and keeps waiting for crumbs to fall from their table. His view of the past is no different from that of the Vishwa Hindu Parishad, Rashtriya Swayamsevak Sangh and their numerous outfits consisting of rowdies and goons who burn books that do not endorse their view, vandalize art objects which they consider blasphemous, present a distorted view of Indian history, and nurture a culture of intolerance. These elements demanded my arrest when my work on beef eating was published, and censured James Laine when his book on Shivaji came out. It is not unlikely that Shourie functions in perfect harmony with them and persons like Dina Nath Batra who targeted A.K. Ramanujan's essay emphasizing the diversity of the Ramayana tradition; Wendy Doniger's writings, which provided an alternative view of Hinduism; Megha Kumar's work on communalism and sexual violence in Ahmadabad since 1969; and Sekhar Bandopadhyaya's textbook on modern India which does not eulogize the RSS.

Arun Shourie seems to have inaugurated a fresh round of battle by reproducing in a second edition his faked, falsified and fabricated historical evidence, thus providing grist to the reactionary mill of Batras and their ilk.

APPENDICES

APPENDIX 1

The Beef-eaters of Ancient India* (Book Review)

WENDY DONIGER

THE ONLY SHOCKING thing about this book is the news that someone has found it shocking – has been 'shocked, shocked' (as Claude Raines would have said) by the argument that people used to eat cows in ancient India. *The Myth of the Holy Cow* is a dry, straight academic survey of the history of Sanskrit texts dealing with the eating, or not-eating, of cows. The author, Dwijendra Narayan Jha, Professor of History at the University of Delhi, has marshalled indisputable evidence proving what every scholar of India has known for well over a century:

(1) In ancient India, from the time of the oldest sacred text, the *Rigveda* (*c.* 1000 BC), cows were eaten regularly, both ritually and for many of the same reasons that people nowadays eat Big Macs ('I eat beef, as long as it is juicy', said a great Vedic sage, Yajnavalkya, in about 900 BC).

(2) Almost as early, the practice of vegetarianism in general, and, somewhat later, the prohibition of beef-eating in particular, spread throughout India, in Buddhism and

*Reprinted from *The Times Literary Supplement*, 8 January 2002.

Jainism as well as in Hinduism, and continued alongside an on-going practice of meat-eating.
(3) Several reformers, most famously Gandhi, made vegetarianism a central tenet of Hinduism.

Nothing shocking here. Yet the dust jacket of the book proudly proclaims: 'A Book the Government of India Demands be Ritually Burned', and the blurb assures us that the book has been 'banned by the Hyderabad Civil Court and the author's life has been threatened'. The *Observer* likened the book's reception to that of Salman Rushdie's *Satanic Verses*, and even the more-PC-than-thou Lingua Franca tells us that the book 'was pulled from the country's shelves'. Why?

The belief that the Hindus have sacred cows is attested in no less an authority than the OED, which defines the term as, primarily, designating 'The cow as an object of veneration amongst Hindus', and cites an 1891 reference from Rudyard Kipling's father, already in the context of Hindu-Muslim conflict ('J.L. Kipling Beast & Man in India vi. 116 The Muhammedan . . . creed is in opposition to theirs and there are rankling memories of a thousand insults to it wrought on the sacred cow.') But the term soon became a global metaphor, indeed a backhanded anti-Hindu ethnic slur, designating precisely the sort of fanaticism that has dogged Professor Jha's book. In US journalism the word came to mean 'someone who must not be criticized', and in American literature, 'an idea, institution, etc., unreasonably held to be immune from questioning or criticism', a sense in which Margaret Mitchell used it in 1936 in *Gone with the Wind* ('I think of my brother, living among the sacred cows of Charleston, and most reverent towards them'). The present Right-wing BJP government, in its fanatical pursuit of 'Hindutva' (literally, 'Hindu-tion'), has ignored the figurative usages that characterize its own methods and attempted to use the alleged literal sanctity of the cow to disenfranchise Muslims, some of whom eat beef and/or slaughter the cows that many Hindus eat. This is apparently what makes this a shocking book: it contradicts the party line, which is that We Hindus have always been here in India, and have Never Eaten Cow; those Muslims have come in, and Kill and Eat Cows, and therefore must be destroyed. The Hindutva argument resembles in many respects the old 'they-are-eating-our-children-and-poisoning-our-wells' accusation, which, as Carlo Ginzburg has demonstrated, was levelled not just against the witches in Europe but, long before that, by the Christians against the Jews, the Romans against the Christians, and the Jews against various enemies.

Since the human species is by nature carnivorous, what is surprising is that there ever were vegetarians, not that we were all, once, meat-eaters, and many of us still are. It is one of the ironies of history that the British, who called themselves Beef-eaters, ruled India. Yet the ancient inhabitants of India resembled nineteenth-century Texans as much as Victorian Britons: the people of the *Rigveda* (like other members of the Indo-European family) were cattle-herders and cattle-rustlers, who went about stealing other peoples' cows and pretending to be taking them back, all in the service of a religion that argued for Lebensraum, constant expansion, more and more grazing land for their horses. They sacrificed cows to the gods and ate them, and counted their wealth in *pashus* (cattle), cognate with Latin *pecus* (as in 'impecunious') and Spanish *pecos* (as in 'Pecos Bill').

The idea of a 'sacred cow' is an Irish bull (the old British chauvinist term for an oxymoron). The word 'sacred' is in any case a Christian term that can be, at best, vaguely and inadequately applied in India, but cows would not in any case qualify for the adjective: there are no cow-goddesses or temples to cows, or icons of cows to which worship is offered, though there are festivals in which people decorate cows and give them fruit and flowers. Since cows are not deities, there is no need for cow statues, as, unlike deities, cows are always visibly present on earth. Benign bulls are beautifully depicted at the doors of Shiva temples, and there are temples to monkeys, tiger temples, temple elephants, shrines to snakes, and even a temple or two to dogs, who are closely associated with Bhairava (an aspect of Shiva), though dogs are as unclean to caste-minded Hindus as pigs are to orthodox Jews. Cows are, in fact, one of the few animals that are not the object of worship in India. Yet cows have been, for centuries, cultural symbols of non-violence and of the passive, bovine aspect of women, in sharp contrast with mares, whom the mythology depicts as over-sexed, insatiable and fatally attractive.

Professor Jha traces the history of the doctrine forbidding the eating of cows or the killing of cows, soundly and thoroughly covering both the classic texts and cutting-edge scholarship, Indian and European, but his arguments are not always as nuanced as they might be. 'Holy' (or 'sacred') means a lot more than not-to-be-killed. Few of us kill, or eat, our children, but none would argue that they are sacred. Eating meat in sacrifice is not the same as eating meat for dinner, and killing, too, can be dichotomized in this way: the great Hindu law-book by Manu argued that: 'The Self-existent One himself created sacrificial animals for sacrifice; sacrifice is for the good of this whole universe; and therefore killing in a sacrifice is not killing.'

To this day it is often argued in India that the meat of animals killed for the table is poison because such animals die in fear and anger, while animals killed for sacrifice are happy to die, and so their meat is sweet. This is a very old way of combating guilt; the myth of the cow who willingly offers not only her milk but her flesh to be eaten is attested in the *Jaiminiya Brahmana*, *c.* 900 BC, which also imagines humans soundlessly screaming while they are being eaten in the other world, in punishment for eating, in this world, not only animals but plants – if they have not been consecrated for sacrifice. More often, however, the cow is singled out for special treatment precisely because she is an animal that you can eat (in the form of her milk) without killing her; the Hindu parallel to the cornucopia (or the German 'Tischlein deck dich') is the myth of the wishing-cow, from whom you can milk anything you desire – not just food but silk cloths, armies of soldiers, anything.

The issue is further complicated by the concept of ahimsa, often translated as 'non-injury' – a concept that Gandhi, in particular, made world-famous – but more literally, 'the absence of the desire to injure or kill'. Ahimsa represents not a political doctrine or even a social theory, but the emotion of the horror of killing, which we have seen attested in 900 BC. Vegetarianism and compassion for animals are not the same thing at all; vegetarianism does not equal 'non-injury'.

It is usual for most individuals to eat meat without killing animals (most non-vegetarians, few of whom hunt or butcher, do it every day) and equally normal for an individual to kill without eating meat (what percentage of hit-men or soldiers devour their fallen enemies?) Indeed, Jan Heesterman has suggested that vegetarianism and killing went hand in hand: that in the earliest period of Indian civilization, meat-eating householders would, in time of war, consecrate themselves as warriors by giving up the eating of meat. They either ate meat or killed. In later Hinduism, the strictures against eating and killing continued to work at odds, so that it was regarded as better (for most people, in general: the rules would vary according to the caste status of the person in each case) to kill an Untouchable than to kill a Brahmin, but better to eat a Brahmin (presuming that one came across a dead one) than to eat an Untouchable (under the same circumstances). It makes a difference if you find the meat already killed or have to kill it, and this would apply not only to Brahmins *vs* Untouchables but to cows *vs* dogs as road-kill.

Nevertheless, the logical assumption that any animal that

one ate had to have been killed by someone led to a natural association between the ideal of vegetarianism and the ideal of non-violence toward living creatures. And this ideal came to prevail in India, reinforced by the idea of reincarnation and its implication that humans and animals were part of a single system of the recycling of souls: do not kill/eat an animal, for it might be your grandmother, or your grandchild, or you. For you are whom you ate, and you may become whom you eat. Food taboos of this sort come in all shapes and sizes in India: there are vegetarians, vegans, people who eat chicken or fish or eggs but not beef, who eat beef as long as it is disguised as curry but not when served as a rare rib roast, or do not drink milk, and so forth.

The lawbooks and their commentaries obsessively count the angels on the head of a roasting skewer. And when we fold this mix back into the broader issues, we must distinguish killing, tormenting (for Hindus will often treat cows in ways that soft-hearted Americans – who eat beef – regard as very cruel indeed), sacrificing, eating and, finally, worshipping, which is quite another issue and, as we have seen, not relevant to Hindu cows at all. Jha doesn't sort all of this out, but it really doesn't matter. His basic point stands and is proved beyond dispute: the claim that Hindus have never eaten cows is false.

But what is the relevance of history? If we could prove that human sacrifice was attested in the *Rigveda* (and humans were, at least theoretically, included in the list of sacrificial victims or *pashus*, along with horses, cows, goats and sheep), would that justify cannibalism today? Not logically or legally, but to a certain type of reactionary religious mind, it would indeed; the past is a very important template for the present; we must do in the present what our ancestors did in *illo tempore*, as Mircea Eliade taught us to call it. And so this sort of historical study does indeed hit the BJP where it hurts.

But who will listen? Who cares? Will any of the people

making the Hindutva arguments – which are not historical or scholarly but religious and political – read Professor Jha's book, or even the TLS review of it? Michel Foucault and Edward Said, among others, have taught us that scholarship is often deeply implicated in creating the political mess in the first place, but scholarship has demonstrated far less power to clean the mess up; like the sorcerer's apprentice, or Frankenstein, or the scientists on the Manhattan Project, scholars create imperialist monsters that they cannot control but merely watch, aghast, from the sidelines, crying, 'No, no, put it down!' Scholars lack all conviction, while ideologues are full of passionate intensity. Yet the fact that *The Myth of the Holy Cow* has been attacked is a good sign, a sign that someone among those thugs in the government reads, and worries that the pen may still be, if not mightier than the nuclear arsenal, at least a weapon worth scanning for, like knives at airports, a weapon capable of subversion.

APPENDIX 2

Saffron Gastronomy*

SUSAN WATKINS

D.N. Jha, The Myth of the Holy Cow
LONDON AND NEW YORK: VERSO, 2002, £16, HARDBACK
183 PP, 1 85984 676 9

THAT JESUS ROAMED the Himalayas, absorbing Vedic wisdom from the gurus he encountered; that the human race originated in Tibet; that the gods reside in the body of the cow, mother of us all – all this has long been taught as established fact in the 20,000 Vidya Bharati schools run under the auspices of the Sangh Parivar, the hardline Hindu-nationalist network that lies behind India's ruling party, the BJP. The Vidya Bharati agenda has already been introduced into primary and secondary schools in BJP-run states, where education policy is often a pawn in coalition deals with regional parties. In 2001, the Sangh-dominated National Council of Educational Research and Training began deleting and rewriting sections of the history textbooks – removing, among other things, any reference to Indian traditions of eating beef. In January 2002, NCERT produced a new history syllabus, founded on its 'value-based'

*Reprinted from *New Left Review*, September-October 2002.

national curriculum framework for the country's schools, which had proposed introducing courses on Vedic mathematics and a 'spirituality quotient' as a form of academic assessment. On 12 September 2002, the Supreme Court set its seal on the new policy, rejecting the contention that the education system was being 'saffronized' with the dismissal of a petition brought against it by a group of educationalists. Prime Minister Vajpayee, schmoozing with Indian millionaires in New York, greeted the decision with glee – adding, for domestic consumption.

'And if saffronization is taking place, what's wrong with that? Bhagwa is a good colour, long associated with the battlefields.' The opposition Congress party announced that it had 'no legal problem' with the judgement.

The teaching of history in post-Independence India, the revisionists argue, has been too 'Westernized' – dominated by the 'children of Macaulay'. Instead, they propose to develop 'a sense of belonging in every individual learner', by focusing on 'India's contribution to world civilization'. The Vidya Bharati narrative that this ambition threatens to draw from is a genuinely postmodern fiction, seamlessly conflating mythology and fact. The Aryan race, indigenous to India, is the nucleus of its proud culture. During the golden age of the Vedic period, the country was the envy of the world; its trade networks spread across the globe, and foreign markets were filled with Indian goods. Its treasure chests flowed with jewels, silver and gold. Marauders and barbarians have always viewed the country with greedy eyes. Bacchus and Dionysus were among the first invaders – they suffered such a crushing defeat that Ancient Greece quaked with terror. After the rout of Darius, Iran could never raise its eyes to India again. Alexander the Great had to beg for Puru's forgiveness.

But Buddhist influence, and the non-violent doctrine of ahimsa, weakened the kingdom. Cowardice spread throughout the land. Since the state bore the burden of filling the monks' begging bowls, the Buddhists gained many recruits. The troops guarding the borders grew listless as army morale was sapped. Arab aggressors, sword in hand, imposed their religion, destroying books and temples, humiliating mothers and sisters. Practices of child marriage, jauhar, sati and purdah were defences against Muslim rapaciousness. Under the Moghuls, the country was divided into two classes: minority Muslim rulers, and the vast majority, the long-suffering Hindus, constantly oppressed.

At stake is the creation of a monolithic national narrative, focused around the supposed essence of Hinduism, an unchanging Brahmanical core. The complex social history of the priestly caste – its mutations through the millennia, its class character and the numerous challenges to its hegemony – is drowned out by shrill proclamations of innate Brahmanical purity, of which vegetarianism and, in particular, the immemorial sanctity of the cow are important aspects. The actual treatment of India's often lame and rackribbed bovine population – bumbling between the Hyundais and Toyotas, or browsing on street-corner rubbish heaps – is not the issue. As last year's protests by outraged customers at the Mumbai McDonald's make clear, it is the ancient link with Hindu purity that counts.

Yet as Dwijendra Narayan Jha's new work reveals, the connexion is far less ancient than it seems. In contrast to many of the revisionists, Jha has studied the Vedic writings in detail – as his thicket of footnotes reveals – as well as surveying a far wider body of textual and archaeological data. His book – the subject of initial banning orders and ritual burnings – is a welcome addition to a growing body of literature that gives a far more complex picture of ancient India. To the Aryan-speaking, semi-nomadic pastoralists who migrated to northwest India from the area of present-day Iran – and whose prayers and chants are recorded in the earliest extant document of the Subcontinent, the *Rigveda*, dating from between 1500 and

1000 BC – the cow was neither sacred nor unslayable. The Aryans' gods – combining, it seems, some of the Avesta deities of Iran, strong-armed Indra and fiery Agni, with the mother goddess and Horned Being of the Indus valley – were particularly partial to offerings of roast ox, goat and beef. Animal sacrifice was a crucial element of their religion. Cattle were also valued for their leather, which was worked up into elaborate trappings for the Aryans' chariots – important symbols of power in a mobile, pastoral world.

The textual evidence for this period relates essentially to northern India. But archaeological excavations have revealed charred and cut cattle bones from virtually all parts of the Subcontinent, suggesting that the consumption of beef, along with mutton, goat, ox and various fowls and fish, was fairly commonplace. At Hastinapura – the ancient capital of the Mahabharata, north of Delhi – bone fragments of sheep, buffalo, goat, pig, elephant and short-horned cattle have been found, many of them cut or charred, and dating from the eleventh to the third century BC. The social universe of the sprawling epic – its original nucleus generated around 800 BC – is exuberantly non-vegetarian. One section – the Vanaparvan – recounts the daily slaughter of two thousand cows in the kitchens of King Rantideva, renowned for distributing vast quantities of beef and grain to his brahmans. The *Ramayana*, too, contains numerous references to the killing of cattle, both for sacrifice and for food: as she is ferried across the Yamuna, Sita vows to sacrifice a thousand cows and a hundred jars of wine to the river, if Rama keeps his vows.

The later Vedic texts, products of the settled agrarian communities around the Ganga-Yamuna doab, provide detailed descriptions of cattle sacrifice, and make clear that humans (as well as gods) consumed the results. As the *Satapatha Brahmana* comments: 'meat is the best kind of food'. Beef should not only be served to honour important guests or to celebrate a new house, but on far more banal occasions: according to Upanishadic precept a veal stew, served with rice and ghee, could ensure a father the happiness of a long-lived, learned son. That cows were highly valued, a symbol of riches, is not, Jha argues, synonymous with their being either sacred or unslayable.

On the other hand, with the beginnings of caste stratification and mercantile development, there is evidence to suggest that the brahman's cattle began to acquire a certain degree of inviolability at this time. The cow was the preferred form of daksina, or sacrificial fee, paid to the priest, and the later Vedic texts warn of the dire consequences that might befall those who injure or misappropriate the brahman's kine. 'O king,' cautions the *Atharvaveda*, 'the gods did not give that cow to you to eat. O warrior, do not eat the brahman's cow, she is not to be eaten.' Such passages should perhaps be seen as brahmanical attempts to assert the hegemony of the priestly caste against kshatriya challenges from below. The emergence in the sixth and fifth centuries BC of anti-brahmanical and anti-caste sects and movements – Buddhism and Jainism pre-eminent among them – would seem further indicators of such tensions. Both were founded by members of the kshatriya, or warrior caste. Buddhism tended to draw its followers from the mercantile, farming and artisan layers, Jainism from the trading and financial elite. A strength of Jha's work is that his analysis of early brahmanical attitudes is integrated into this wider panorama of Indian practice.

Both Buddhism and Jainism were resolutely opposed to animal sacrifice, and there are many stories of the Buddha counselling brahmans against it. The principle of 'right action' included abstaining from the conscious destruction of any sentient being, while the principle of 'right speech' is illustrated by the protests of the ox, Nandivisala, against the abusive language of his brahman master. Nevertheless, as Jha points out, the Middle Path soon acknowledged the 'three blameless ways' of eating meat – the beast's slaughter need only be 'unseen, unheard or unsuspected'; in a broadening of the Path, the three were later increased to nine. Among these, presumably, were the contents of the Buddha's last supper, a vexed subject for his followers; although the *Milindapanho* assures us that he did not die from the pork itself, which was 'in good condition, light, pleasant, full of flavour and fine for the digestion', but from 'the extreme weakness of his body'. While the scornful Jains accused the Buddhists of regarding as pure anything that fell into their begging bowls, in practice they too discovered exceptions to the rule of non-slaughter: Jain monks who found themselves in a deserted village, or a settlement of robbers, where meat was the only food on offer, were permitted to tuck in with the rest.

It was not easy to curb the varied appetites of the subcontinent by priestly precept. The edicts of the third-century BC King Ashoka, himself a Buddhist, which prohibited the slaughter of a long list of animals throughout the Mauryan empire – stretching from present-day Afghanistan to Karnataka in the far south – appear to have been ignored; not least in the royal kitchens, where two peacocks and a deer were dished up every day. While the Mauryan court's brahman adviser Kautilya also proscribed the killing of calves, bulls and milch cows, he fixed the fine for such offences at a nominal 50 panas, and still managed to recommend the salutary effects of cow bones as manure.

The legal codes of ancient India are equally equivocal. That of Manu, compiled between 200 BC and 200 AD, sanctions meat-eating in honour of the gods or important guests – indeed, the brahman who refuses consecrated flesh is condemned to be reborn as a beast for twenty-one existences – while condemning it in less exalted contexts. Manu's code recognized five major sins: first, killing a brahman; second, stealing; third, drinking liquor; fourth, having sexual intercourse with a guru's wife; fifth, associating with those guilty of any of the above. Cow slaughter, however, did not feature on the list. Sanskrit medical treatises of the same period are markedly pragmatic. The renowned compilation of Caraka (first-second century AD) prescribes a gruel of beef gravy sharpened with pomegranate juice for fevers, and Susruta (third-fourth century AD) recommends the meat for coughs, catarrhs and 'a morbid craving for food'. Secular literature provides a host of similar references right up to the eighteenth century.

Jha argues, nevertheless, for a distinct shift in attitudes towards the cow, at least in northern India, from around the middle of the first millennium AD. This period – characterized by warring kingly states, social and political instability, a catastrophic decline in trade, the emergence of land as the primary source of wealth and the consolidation of large landholdings by an important brahmanical layer – was understood at the time as the age of Kali, of destruction or decay, necessitating deep changes in social mores. It saw the transition from a sacrificial to an image-based religion, more appropriate to the *kaliyuga*, with the incorporation of the cults of Shiva, Vishnu, and their *avatars* – the classic Hindu pantheon. The transformation, however, affected the gods rather than the priests. The epoch witnessed the reassertion of brahmanical authority, the emergence of an orthodox Vedanta school of thought, triumphing over its rivals, and the re-writing of the bardic epics as sacrosanct texts.

During the *kaliyuga*, mores acknowledged to have been appropriate in earlier, less troubled times – beef-eating among them – were now condemned, especially when practised by lower castes. In normative literature, the brahman's life and possessions were now consistently represented as more valuable than those of other caste categories. Narratives in several different genres elaborate on the dire consequences of defying these rules – kings who humiliate brahmans invariably come to no good. It seems likely that such grim reiterations were necessitated by a social reality in which brahmanical ideals were actively contested. It is in this context that the cow was co-opted into the survival strategies of the priestly elite.

Yet privilege should not be mistaken for uniform dominance: even within Hinduism – let alone the many other traditions – a wide variety of religious and dietary practices have persisted down to the present day. Jha's fascinating book inevitably tells only a fraction of the story. The vast and complex history of the south, the northeast, the tribal areas and forest regions has still barely begun to be explored. The origins of the current 'Hinduization' of Indian culture, asserting a continuity with a monolithic, unbroken tradition, lie not in the ancient Vedas but in the colonialist confections of nineteenth-century European Indologists who, with their own conceptions of the Aryan race, focused their attentions upon the Sanskrit texts, scanting the many other regional traditions whose languages they did not know. The concept of an essentially 'Hindu' India was a product of modernity – of tensions induced by the demands of an industrial-capitalist occupying power.

Mass mobilizations around the slogan of the 'holy cow' are a graphic representation of this, as recent scholarship by Gyan Pandey and others has revealed. The first Gaurakshini Sabhas – Cow Protection Societies – were launched by the Hindu Arya Samaj in 1882. A network of local groups was established across north and central India in the following decades, targeting not the British authorities but local Muslim communities as source of their ills. Leading donors to the Gaurakshini Sabhas were often big landowners, bankers and traders; local zamindari landlords, facing declining agricultural returns, sought to hegemonize their recalcitrant tenantry on a communalist basis; priests saw an opportunity to re-establish their spiritual ascendancy; in an age of growing social insecurity and increasing levels of exploitation, a new layer of clerks and petty bureaucrats, undervalued inter-mediaries between the colonial administration and the populace, found an outlet for the unbearable tensions of their lot; rising castes, seen as only marginally 'clean', could assert a fuller purity by loudly demonstrating their piety on the question of the cow; fakirs and swamis played an essential role. The inept or opportunist decisions of the colonialist authorities – bending now to one reactionary authority, now another, in the name of an 'established usage' that they themselves had overthrown – provided innumerable causes for dispute. The result was a series of provocations – Muslim butchers, herding cows to a wedding feast, beaten or killed, and their kine appropriated – rising to communally incited slaughter before the celebrations of Baqr-Id in Maunath Bhanjan in 1893, of a sort that would pave the way for the disaster of Partition.

There are obvious parallels with the present day. The current hinduization of the curriculum – the stress on 'India's contribution to world civilization', while rigorously stamping out any sense of other civilizations' contributions to India – also comes at a time of intense pressure from outside, with the country thrown wide open to the manipulations of international capital; a drastic reversal, in terms of the self-sufficiency of the Nehru years. While state universities exhibit the symptoms of advanced malnutrition, extra funds have been provided for kamarkanda courses to produce certified priests. The expansion of an elite layer of private education – spared the yoga courses and spirituality quotient – has been forcefully promoted by the World Bank. The recent Ambani report on private investment in education enthuses about the possibility of creating a 'competitive, yet co-operative, knowledge-based society', an environment that 'does not produce industrial workers and labourers but fosters [cutting-edge] knowledge workers . . . placing India in the vanguard of the information age'. Funds from the social sciences, in other words, are to be shifted to

IT, to fill the niche in the global market for highly trained software technicians. The scenario is uncannily reminiscent of the British government's Hunter Commission report of 1882, which recommended a switch to technical training for the Indians, on the grounds that liberal education was threaten- ing to produce a critical native intelligentsia, whose thoughts might tend to national independence.

What is abandoned in the NCERT proposals is any concept of education as rational endeavour, or methodologically guided inquiry into the unknown. It could be interesting to introduce Vedic 'maths' into a comparative history of methods of mental arithmetic; to memorize the Sanskrit shlokas off by heart is another story. Many of the wildest claims for a martial Hindu civilization come from the websites of NRIs – the enormous Indian diaspora whose wealth and influence, within whichever niche of the domestic class system they hail from, is vastly amplified by their residence abroad. For computer scientists, engineers, investment bankers or development advisers in Buffalo, Manhattan or Des Moines, a Vedic capsule swallowed twice daily may be exactly the required boost for identity-deficiency levels, allowing for a homely sense of smugness as one chooses Chicken McNuggets over Big Mac. But – faced with a complex, uneven, rapidly evolving social reality – it ill equips the mass of India's children to articulate their own collective needs.

APPENDIX 3

Frontline Interview

By
AJOY ASHIRWAD MAHAPRASHASTA

VOL. 26, ISSUE 25, 5-18 DECEMBER 2009

DWIJENDRA NARAYAN JHA, an eminent historian, has campaigned extensively against the communalisation of history. His book *Myth of the Holy Cow*, wherein he dispelled popular misconceptions that Muslims introduced beef-eating in India, created ripples in political circles. An ardent critic of the Hindu nationalist ideology, Jha, along with three other historians, sought to prove in a report, *Ramjanmabhoomi-Babri Masjid: A Historians' Report to the Nation*, that there was no evidence of the existence of a Ram temple under the Babri mosque and that the controversy was created by the Sangh Parivar for political gains. In an interview to *Frontline*, he talks about his findings in Ayodhya and the role of professional historians in countering hate politics for a better nation-building process. Excerpts:

With the Liberhan Commission's report indicting several top and second-rung leaders of the Sangh Parivar, what will be the status of the original Babri Masjid-Ram Janmabhoomi dispute?

Well, in my view, this has no bearing on the original dispute. I have seen the ATR [Action Taken Report] and I didn't find anything there that has any implication for what will happen to the dispute. The Liberhan report doesn't talk about the original dispute. That matter is still pending in court. I think there should be a day-to-day trial, and the judiciary should expedite the whole matter now that the report is out. Those who have been named should be brought to court; but my own feeling is that the Government of India does not seem enthusiastic about taking action against any of those who are named in the list of 68 people.

Justice M.S. Liberhan has also said that the Muslim organisations failed to protect the interests of the people they claimed to represent. How valid is this opinion?

That would be a very remote conclusion one can draw. You see fundamentalism of all sorts. Maybe some Muslim organisations have heightened the consciousness of the community to protect the monument, but that's about all. But if you say that these organisations gave implicit instigation to convert people to fundamentalism, I don't think so.

Could you briefly tell us about the findings of the independent report prepared by M. Athar Ali, Suraj Bhan, R.S. Sharma and you?

The Babri Masjid was built by Mir Baqi, a military officer in the kingdom of the Mughal ruler Babur, in 1528-9. The main contention of the Sangh Parivar is that the mosque was built by demolishing a Ram temple and that it was the birthplace of Rama. But it was only in 1948-9 that you see a miraculous appearance of idols under Gobind Ballabh Pant's chief ministership [of the United Provinces] and Nehru's prime ministership. Between then and the mid-1970s, one does not hear of this controversy at all. It was only after the VHP [Vishwa Hindu Parishad] came into being that it started talking about Kashi, Mathura and Ayodhya as pilgrimage centres. Gradually in 1986, you see the opening of the locks [of the masjid] and, subsequently, the *shilanyaas*.

All these developments coincided with the emergence of the VHP as a strong force and other organisations such as the Bajrang Dal and the RSS [Rashtriya Swayamsevak Sangh] in the Hindutva camp. They made political use of it.

I think the dispute is really an artefact created by the Hindutva camp for fundamentalist purposes that culminated in the demolition of the mosque in 1992. Before 1992, slogans like 'Mandir wohin banayenge', and 'this is Ram's *janmabhoomi* [birthplace]' rent the air in North India. But if you look at the historical texts and evidence, Ram Janmabhoomi does not find prominence.

For instance, a very important text, *Skanda Purana*, speaks of Ayodhya *mahatmya* [greatness]. Only 100 verses are devoted to the ascent of Rama to heaven from a place called Swargadwar at the confluence of the river Ghaggar and the river Saryu. It exists even now. But only 10 verses are devoted to his birth. This shows that his birthplace was not important but what was important was the place from where he went to heaven. Only Swargadwar was a *tirtha* (centre of pilgrimage). In the 11th century text *Krtyakalpataru* by Bhatta Lakshmi Dhar, the list of pilgrimages is detailed extensively. It is a very long list. The author was a minister in the Gahrwal kingdom, which ruled even Ayodhya at that time. He does not mention Ayodhya as a centre for pilgrimage in 'Tirthavivechan Kanda' [a section devoted to pilgrimage centres in the book].

Now, take, for instance, Tulsidas, the author of *Ramacharitamanas*. He writes about Rama and Ayodhya but never says that a Rama temple was demolished. I don't understand why these people made so much of hullabaloo about the temple.

Other types of archaeological evidence also show that in the whole of North India, there were no temples exclusively devoted to Rama until the late 17th-early 18th century. In South India, you find them since the Chola period (10th-12th century) but not in North India. Two or three temples of Rama belonging to the 12th century are found in Madhya Pradesh but not in Uttar Pradesh, not in Bihar, not even in Orissa. Ram temples became common in North India only in the 17th century.

The famous temple devoted to Sita at Janakpur in Nepal Tarai came up only in the late 18th-early 19th century. I don't think there is enough historical evidence about the temple. In fact Ayodhya was important for other religions, such as Jainism and Buddhism. The Chinese pilgrim Xuan Zhang [who toured the subcontinent during the Gupta period, around AD 630] recorded that there were around 100 Buddhist monasteries and only 10 abodes of *devas* [brahmanical gods]. *Vishnu Smriti* also lists 52 pilgrim centres very early in 3rd-4th century AD but it does not name Ayodhya. What I am trying to say, even for argument's sake, is that if there was a temple so important at Ayodhya, it should have existed in the literary and archaeological evidence before 1528 when the mosque was built.

At least, it should have existed in the 11th-12th century.

Before the demolition of the masjid, Professor B.B. Lal of the Archaeological Survey of India had claimed to have found 'evidence of pillar bases' of a mandir beneath the Babri Masjid. Indologist Koenraad Elst also writes about the [existence of a] temple. Some have said that the mosque was called Masjid-e-janmasthaan. What is, then, the basis of such claims?

B.B. Lal in his first report on Ayodhya did not mention any temple. He says that the upper-most layers are represented by Kankar [stone] and other things. In 1985-6 he retired from the ASI and began to change his tune. He began to say that the pillars of the mosque might indicate a pre-existing temple. But that was all tongue-in-cheek. Then, subsequently, in a paper he presented [at a seminar] in Patna he said that he had not found any evidence of a Rama temple at Ayodhya and urged Mother Earth to forgive him for this. Later on, at another seminar in Vijaywada, he said that the only way to solve the problem was to excavate the area, which meant demolishing the mosque. He and his camp started saying that something should be done to demolish the mosque. There was already the PWD's [Public Works Department] levelling work and kar seva going on there.

Archaeology is a scientific activity and cannot be done like this. The pillars are, in fact, 1.70 metres in height and the experts who went with us to visit the site said that these pillars could not be load-bearing pillars. The mosque had three big domes and the height of the 14 pillars did not suggest that they were part of a temple. What may have happened is that they could have been brought from outside for decorative purposes. What is important is that the area does not have that kind of pillar stone. The art historians whom we consulted said that these pillars could be from Bengal and must have been brought by the Palas who ruled the area.

Even the word *janmasthaan* does not exist in any of the texts. *Skanda Purana* is an amorphous text and its composition stretches over centuries, from the 14th century to the 18th century. It is only in the last stage [around the 18th century] that *janmasthaan* is mentioned in passing. So, the whole idea becomes important only in the 19th century. There were conflicts, of course, but there is no evidence to support them. It is important to see that in the earlier period, we do not get any sculptures from Ayodhya. There are two or three catalogues in museums in Uttar Pradesh. One in Lucknow, one in Allahabad and one in Faizabad, which is Ayodhya. None of the catalogues mentions Rama.

The VHP movement around the Ram temple started only in the 1970s after the Paramhans vs *Wakf Board case. How did Ayodhya become a centre of contention? Does colonial knowledge formation play a part in the controversy as some historians try to suggest?*

The British might have had something to do with this. But in Ayodhya, there were around 6,000 temples in the 19th and the early 20th century. It is likely that there were property disputes like the Wakf Board and the Paramhans court case. Such court cases might be a legacy of the past. Even if the Britishers played a role, how does it matter? It could have been their method of governance, instigating the existing conflicts. The point is that there was no temple.

The VHP and leaders like Pravin Togadia have given an estimate of around 30,000 temple sites where mosques came up in India. Temple politics such as the Ayodhya case has had a calamitous impact on national contemporary politics, leading to killings and riots in the past two decades. The American historian Richard M. Eaton's Essays on Islam and Indian History *is probably the only book that studies the temple desecration issue and pegs the number of desecrated temples at 80 between 1192 and 1760 as a consequence of political compulsion and not because of religious righteousness. As a historian, do you see the need for more such studies to counter the growing fascist influence on history writing?*

Yes, of course. This will ultimately help to unite different religious communities and help in nation building. How do people like Togadia come up with such a figure? If historians take up such studies it will reduce the much-hyped hostilities. Togadia and others speak of Muslim hostility towards Hindus. But what happened in Karnataka? Lingayats occupied Jain temples. They put their *tilak* [a Hindu symbol] on Jain statues, appropriated other religious places of worship. In fact, Jains were so much oppressed by the Lingayats that they had to seek protection from the Vijaynagara rulers. In Tamil Nadu, 8,000 Jains were impaled at a Madurai court, as mentioned in a historical text. It is not only Muslims who did it. This has been done by all religions. Similar things happened in Europe also. Churches were damaged by Muslims. Sects within Christianity fought against each other. We always say that Hinduism is the most tolerant. If there is anything like the Hindu, there is a streak of intolerance in all historical texts. Vaishnavas and Shaivites have fought all the time.

As was understood in Ayodhya and now at many other places in India, a disputed structure has many meanings and emotions attached to it – religious, territorial, property, class and caste. In your view what is a disputed structure and what are its political implications?

The common people are not bothered about these disputes. There is a class understanding to it. When we went to Ayodhya, we didn't find any Muslim or Hindu living there who was interested in the controversy. Kar sevaks were mobilised from outside and used for political purposes. What I am saying is that if there is a disputed structure anywhere and the local people are not bothered, the state should see to it that it does not flare up. Only those who belong to the elite and who are likely to gain something out of the conflict are interested. How does the state function? They are talking of Rama now. In Delhi itself, there are thousands of Hanuman temples that have come up on illegally occupied government land and the state is not playing any role in stopping it.

Our Constitution identifies religion while defining secularism but it doesn't say that a state official can identify himself as belonging to one religion while doing his duty. When the first President of India, Rajendra Prasad, went to take a dip in the Ganga at Prayag [Allahabad], there was a controversy. People objected to his performing the religious ritual with the presidential paraphernalia. But today, no one objects to such things when the Prime Minister goes to a gurdwara. People are against giving any subsidy for Hajj pilgrimage. But no one questions the huge amount of state money spent at the Vaishno Devi temple [Katara, Jammu & Kashmir] or for the Amarnath Yatra and the Kumbh Mela.

Ayodhya is a clear case of politics that relied heavily on the study of historical 'facts'. What is a historical fact and how should the state look at it in the methods of governance? Even the state is following different secular trajectories. Liberhan has quoted Amartya Sen while pushing the values of secularism, in a way keeping in line with the 'facts' that have come out of your school of history. In 2003, the same judicial machinery within a nation state implicitly validated the facts of the school of history represented by the likes of B.B. Lal when the Allahabad High Court (Lucknow Bench) ordered a probe to find out about the existence of the temple. How, as a professional historian who is in a position to critique both the state and the communal forces, do you locate yourself in society and how do historians participate in these complexities through history writing, given the complex nature of historical interpretations?

I think historians and social scientists have to come out very clearly and say that there cannot be a state religion, and a nation state cannot be built on the basis of religion. The state should rely on historians and not on what the courts say.

The Allahabad High Court order of excavation was not in good taste because the court doesn't have any academic credentials. Even the ASI's findings are awful. It takes help from Tojo Vikas International, which has no archaeological expertise. It uses the GPR [Ground Penetration Radar], which has nothing to do with archaeology.

Their conclusion is that there are certain anomalies and disturbances under the ground. What does that mean? It is a site 2,000 years old and there can be anomalies for anything like earthquakes or conflicts between different groups or hundreds of reasons.

Archaeological evidence becomes important in their context

of physical relationship to the surroundings in a certain material culture.

In order to resolve the dispute over fact, the best thing is to have B.B. Lal and other historians sit in front of the court and debate. The court could then decide on what convinces it on the basis of rationality. That is one of the ways.

There was a system of *vaad-vivaad* (debate) and *shaastrarth* [interpretation of shastras] in ancient times. The court should take into account the patron-client relationship, like the one B.B. Lal has with the BJP. The Liberhan Commission has recommended setting up a national commission to look into the masjid-mandir dispute, but the Government of India refused to have that, citing the existence of the ASI. My point is: Where was the ASI when the mosque was demolished? I participated in the series of deliberations that took place between the Babri Masjid group and the VHP group, and I always found that the ASI's stand was equivocal. We were given access to antiquities, but the ASI didn't give us the site notebook of Trench 4, which was the crucial evidence for judging whether there was anything underground.

The site notebook is the only record of day-to-day excavation detail as after excavation the ground is filled with earth. There should be an autonomous national commission constituted by historians and archaeologists both from India and outside.

The ASI should be taken away from the Culture Ministry and made a part of the national commission, and, perhaps, statutory if it is required. The ASI should be made accountable to the commission.

There seems to be a gap between history in classrooms and popular historical notions, as is clearly reflected in the Ram Janmabhoomi case. Similarly, the state tries to create its own history as part of nation building and the political parties teach another kind of history for indoctrination. How do you assess the role of a professional historian in engaging with popular history to reshape historical understanding among the masses? Do you see any space in between from where history writing is possible in order to create a harmonious society instead of a divisive one?

I think, in this regard, historians are at fault to a certain extent. If professional historians write for the people that will ultimately have some impact.

In Gujarat, what happened in 2002 can be attributed to the kind of history that was being taught in the State for the past 40 years. In North India, schools like Sishu Mandir and Vidya Bharati are teaching non-history in the name of history.

Ninety per cent of professional historians are the most secular people in the country, but the State has to play a greater role in unifying the education system. Anything that is not borne out by rationality and evidence should be stopped altogether by the State.

The problem, however, is that education is both a Central and a State subject. The NCERT brings out model textbooks, but the States do not adopt them. They make their own changes. Secularisation of education and promotion of scientific temper should be a State effort. Otherwise, whatever historians write, it won't be of any help. I don't see any indication of this in the ATR. The State makes its own compromises according to political pressure, as was seen in the Ram Setu case recently.

Historians who come in proximity to power change their secular lines, too. There should be an atmosphere of dialogue in the academic community. Intellectuals should come out in the open and say that there was no Ram temple in Ayodhya, which most of them believe. They should make their assumptions clear to the reader and then be as objective as possible in writing history. Only then the reader will judge the writer and historical facts better.

APPENDIX 4

Scroll.in Interview

8 SEPTEMBER 2015

EMINENT ANCIENT INDIA historian Prof. D.N. Jha speaks to *Scroll.in* on yet another attempt to push back the *Rigveda* by good many centuries and the motive behind this perennial endeavour of the Rashtriya Swayamsevak Sangh and Right-wing historians.

Towards the end of September, Delhi University's Sanskrit department plans to make public research material which would show that the Rigvedic period lasted from 8000 BC to 5000 BC. What do you think of this exercise?

I am not sure whether the Sanskrit department of Delhi University has the necessary expertise to undertake the responsibility. I was a member of the history faculty for three decades during which I frequently interacted with the members of the Sanskrit department but never met any credible Vedicist. If they indeed had the expertise what prevented them from undertaking the task all these years? Was it necessary to wait for the BJP to come to power with a majority in Parliament? Moreover, the Sanskrit department has already asserted that the Rigvedic period lasted from 8000 BC to 5000 BC. They have stated their conclusion before undertaking the exercise of dating the Vedic texts without waiting for the conclusion! What kind of research is this?

Is there a broad agreement among scholars on the date of the Rigveda? What's the basis of this agreement?

According to the general consensus, the *Rigveda* is dated to around 1500 BC, though its first and last sections are dated later and could be contemporary of the three Vedas – *Sama*, *Yajur* and *Atharva*.

The mention of the Vedic deities in the Mitanni inscription of the 14th century implies that the upper date of the *Rigveda* is not beyond 15th century BC. The Mitanni kingdom was situated in north-west Syria. The Mitanni inscription, dated 1380 BC, records a treaty between a Mitanni king and a Hittite king. It mentions several gods whose names occur in the *Rigveda*. These are: Indara (Indra), Mitras (Mitra), Nasatiya (Nasitya, that is, the Asvins) and Uruvanass (Varuna). This record, among other things, has been used by experts to date the *Rigveda*.

The dating of this text (*Rigveda*) has much to do with determining the traits of the Aryan culture for which one has to depend on the *Zend Avesta* (the text of Zoroastrianism) and Homer's *Iliad*. Its (*Rigveda*) similarity with the *Avesta* and the geographical information contained in it make it necessary to date it in relation to those texts. The close resemblance between the language and culture of the *Avesta* and the *Rigveda* has been noted by many scholars. Examples of words occurring in the *Avesta* and the *Rigveda* are: haoma (soma), daha (dasa), hindu (sindhu), Ahura (Asura), yasna (yajna), etc. This kind of evidence has also been used for dating the *Rigveda*.

The dating of the *Rigveda* would thus draw insights from different disciplines like comparative linguistics, ecology and anthropology and so on.

Isn't there an alternative date for the Rigveda?

The only alternative view of the chronology of the Vedas is that of the Hindu Right. This is based on the traditional astronomical information. This pushes the text's antiquity to the 4th millennium BC but this has been rejected by recent studies.

Is this traditional astronomical information credible?

Frankly, I have not followed closely the studies of the Vedic astronomical references by various scholars. But I know that there is no consensus among them and the dates of the *Rigveda* suggested by them ranges from 11th century BC to 4000 BC. Moreover, the Rigvedic astronomical 'evidence' may be dubious. It may be noted that the Hindu Right treats the Vedas as divinely revealed and having a fantastic antiquity. But this view is not credible at all: the Vedas are not divine in origin, nor can they be assigned the fantastic antiquity. In history it is the evidence that matters, not the faith.

Contrary to the Hindutva propaganda, the generally accepted view so far is that the Vedic culture is later than the Harappan culture. There is no correspondence between the Harappan and the Vedic cultures. The latter is predominantly pastoral and the former is known for its well developed urban features. The Harappan centres amply testify to the existence of crafts and commerce and to the extensive use of burnt bricks but these are absent in the *Rigveda*.

There is also the issue of horse.

The horse and horse-drawn chariot figure prominently in the *Rigveda*: it has been pointed out that the various forms of *ashva* (horse) are mentioned 215 times in the *Rigveda*. But horse is totally absent in the Harappan cultural complex. The presence of horse is a characteristic feature of the Vedic culture which is why the Hindutva scholars (if scholars they can be called!)

have tried to assert, time and again, that horse was known to Harappans: their assertion has been based on what is a piece of faked evidence produced some years ago by one of their champions.

Who produced the fake evidence of horse?

N.S. Rajaram and Natwar Jha produced a computer enhanced seal which they projected as evidence of horse at Harappa and scholars have called it a 'Piltdown horse' (sarcastically named after British Piltdown man, a 1912 hoax which sought to establish the 'missing link' between ape and man), at Harappa. Michael Witzel and Steve Farmer exposed the fraud committed by Rajaram and Jha. (See the October 13, 2000, cover story of *Frontline.*)

You know, non-serious students of history living in the 21st century are unable to imagine how an urban culture lapsed into a pastoral one.

That is a wrong way of looking at the Harappan and the Rigvedic (periods). There was a gap of nearly three centuries between them, though there was also an overlap between the later part of Harappan civilisation and that of the Rigvedic at a few places. The decline of Harappan civilisation has been discussed in detail by many scholars and so has the emergence of the Rigvedic Aryans on the Indian subcontinental scene. The two represent two different historical processes.

Indeed, there are no credible alternative theories to the generally accepted view that the Vedic culture is later than the Harappan culture. The only alternative I can think of is the Hindutva propaganda.

What explains the obsession of rightwing historians to push back the Rigvedic period centuries back?

The main features of the perception of the past as presented by the Right-wing historians appear to be their obsession with the antiquity of Hinduism, and the Vedas from which it is believed to have derived, as well as their obsession with the Hindus being the original inhabitants of India. This has much to do with their anti-Muslim stance. Since Islam came from outside they demonise Muslims as the other. And if they are the other the Hindus have to be the original habitants of the land. From this it follows that the authors of the Harappan culture, the oldest culture of the Indian subcontinent, have to be Hindus. Hence the laboured attempt to project the Harappan culture as Vedic. But this view was not acceptable even to the late R.C. Majumdar, who extended an ideological support to the communal agenda of the Hindu Right. He was the only credible Right-wing historian. N.S. Rajaram and Natwar Jha and their likes among the RSS ideologues are no substitutes for him.

Are the Aryans best described as a race or speakers of the Indo-Aryan language? How did this distinction come about? Why is the Hindu Right so invested in claiming Aryan origins?

In the 19th century the Aryans were often projected both as a racial category as well as speakers of the Indo-Aryan language and the German-born philologist, Max Müller often used race and language as interchangeable categories. With growing awareness of the untenability of race/language equation, the Aryans are no longer considered as a racial category. However, the Hindu Right has clung to the effete and obsolete ideas which derive inspiration from the views of the Theosophical Society, especially its president, Col. Olcott, and Dayananda Saraswati, the founder of the Arya Samaj. Both postulated that the Aryans were indigenous to India and modern Hindus are their descendants, and that the Aryan culture was the cradle of civilisation and the Vedas were the repositories of all knowledge. It is this view that runs across the Hindutva perception all through. The Hindutva-vadis are so obsessed with the Aryan indegenism that they go to ridiculous lengths to assert their position. When Bal Gangadhar Tilak, himself a revivalist, suggested that they came from the Arctic, the RSS Sarsanghchalak or Supreme Leader, M.S. Golwalkar had no hesitation in asserting that the North Pole in those days was located in Bihar/Orissa.

Historians belonging to the Hindu Right often argue that history has been constantly rewritten. They wonder why they can't rethink and revise theories.

No one prevents them from revising theories. But any revision has to be based on evidence. Incessant propaganda cannot be the basis of historical reconstruction; it is a display of ignorance. The reason why the Hindu Right's view is contested is not the ideology but the lack of evidence in whatever they say about the Aryan migration. As of now, the evidence – linguistic and archaeological – points to the migration of the Aryans from the north-west.

There may be many views of the past but the history based on a rigorous analysis of the various types of evidence is more reliable than the one based on riotous imagination.

There are multiple histories or imaginings of the past. So what do we teach schoolchildren? They are bound to get confused listening to different ideas about the past.

As for school textbooks one should emphasise those aspects of the past on which there is a general consensus among historians. Controversial issues, however, may be introduced in higher classes.

If the BJP-RSS were to remain in power for another 10–15 years, do you fear historians might want to rethink their position to please those who rule?

When Hitler was in power many scholars changed their

academic stand, but there were many who migrated to other countries to escape persecution. Although India has entered into Dark Age with Modi coming to power, I don't visualise a situation in which Indian historians will migrate out of India. But it is not unlikely that some of them may dilute their earlier position, to seek favours from the Modi government. In fact, there is no dearth of scholars who always try to please the powers-that-be. Proximity to political power often undermines the honesty of academics.

APPENDIX 5

Frontline Interview

By

AJOY ASHIRWAD MAHAPRASHASTA

VOL. 32, ISSUE 21, 30 OCTOBER 2015

THE ISSUE OF COW slaughter and beef consumption is once again in the eye of a political storm. Hindutva ideologues, aided by the government, have successfully mounted cow-protection programmes across the country and are in the process of using the cow as a political symbol to polarise Hindu and Muslim communities. *Frontline* spoke to D.N. Jha, the eminent historian of ancient and medieval India, on the food practices in India over the centuries and the place of the cow within these systems. Jha has published numerous seminal books on ancient and medieval India.

His books *Holy Cow: Beef in Indian Dietary Traditions* (2002) and *The Myth of the Holy Cow* (2009) drew upon vast historical sources to establish the practice of beef consumption from ancient India onwards, thus dispelling the Hindutva myth that the practice of beef-eating was introduced during Islamic rule in India. His books attracted considerable controversy and Jha also received death threats from Hindu extremists for positing the theory. He explains how popular myths about the cow and beef-eating were systematically etched into the nation's memory by Hindutva extremists and speaks about their larger political interests in rewriting history. Excerpts from an email interview:

What prompted you to take up historical research on the dietary habits of early India? Why does beef-eating become so central an issue in your book?

Since I was interested in the issue of Hindu identity and its relation to food culture, I undertook the research on the early dietary history of India. In the course of my study I found that there was considerable material on beef-eating which could be put together. Also, those were the days when the NDA I [National Democratic Alliance] was in power at the Centre and there was a controversy going on about the mention of beef-eating in NCERT [National Council of Educational Research and Training] textbooks. This prompted me to integrate the relevant data into a book and present it before the reading public. That is why the history of beef-eating became central to the book. But if you read the book you will come across much evidence on the practice of eating the flesh of other animals, too.

The cow has been an important figure in an agrarian economy. Was there any economic logic to cow sacrifices or slaughter in early India?

Cattle sacrifices can be explained in terms of both economic and cultural factors. As you know, the Indo-Aryans migrated to India around the middle of the second millennium BC and they brought along with them several traits of Indo-European life, such as pastoralism, incipient agriculture and religious beliefs and practices including the practice of animal/cattle sacrifice. They also brought with them a number of Indo-Iranian gods (e.g. Indra, Agni, Soma, etc.) for whom sacrifices were made. Since sedentary agriculture had yet to develop, the sacrifice of animals – including cattle – met both dietary and sacrificial requirements. Amongst the gods, Indra had a special liking for bulls and buffaloes and amongst men, the respected sage of Mithila, Yajnavalkya, was fond of cow's flesh.

Are there other historians who have worked on the dietary habits of people in the Vedic age and after? D.D. Kosambi had written about Brahmins eating beef in his book Ancient India.

R.L. Mitra was the first Indian scholar to write on the practice of beef-eating during the Vedic period. Several other scholars, including P.V. Kane and D.D. Kosambi, have referred to it. So I am not the first to write about sacrificial killing of the cow and beef-eating. But unlike other scholars I have argued that beef-eating has continued to remain a part of Indian tradition even after the Vedic period, for which there is considerable evidence.

Could you also cite some historical texts which, according to your research, made it clear that beef-eating had been a normal practice in early and medieval India? Were there instances in early Indian texts where cow 'worship' is also validated?

In my book *The Myth of the Holy Cow*, I have tried to show that far from being a 'baneful bequeathal' of Islam, beef-eating was common in the Vedic period. This is evident from the sacrifices made to the gods, to which there are many references. These are from Vedic as well as post-Vedic texts. At one place in the *Rigveda* (X.86.14), Indra, the greatest of the Vedic gods, is described as stating 'they cook for me fifteen plus twenty oxen'. At other places he is referred to as having eaten the flesh of bulls (X.28.3), of one (X.27.2), or of a hundred buffaloes (VI.17.11) or 300 buffaloes (V.29.7) or a thousand buffaloes (VIII.12.8). Cattle were also sacrificed for Agni, who is described in the *Rigveda* as 'one whose food is ox and the barren cow' (VIII.43.11). Many similar references are available from later Vedic texts and one of them, the *Taittiriya Brahmana*

(III.9.8), unambiguously refers to the sacrificial killing of the cow which is 'verily food'. That the sacrificial victim was generally meant for human consumption is indicated by several texts, especially the *Gopatha Brahmana* (I.3.18), wherein it is stated that the carcass was to be divided into thirty-six shares.

Cattle were killed also in ordinary domestic rites. A Rigvedic passage (X.85.13) refers to the slaughter of a cow on the occasion of marriage, and later, in the *Aitareya Brahmana* (III.4), we are told that 'if a ruler of men comes as a guest or anyone else deserving of honour comes, people kill a cow.

One of the most important occasions for killing a cow was the reception of important guests (*madhuparka*), referred frequently in the Vedic and later texts. Literary references to 'madhuparka' are found till quite late in ancient India. Cattle slaughter was also intimately connected with the cult of the dead and the degree of satisfaction the manes derived from the *shraddha* varied according to the animal offered: the *Apastamba Dharmasutra* speaks of how cow's flesh gratified the *pitris* (dead ancestors) for a year. Thus, there is no doubt that killing of the cow and eating its flesh was quite common in the Vedic and post-Vedic times. The *Brihadaranyaka Upanishad* (VI.4.18) even goes to the ridiculous extent of recommending a diet of veal or beef with rice and ghee to the person desirous of having a learned son.

While there is copious evidence of cow slaughter and beef-eating, there is also much evidence of the cow being treated as riches for which the Vedic people fought wars. As pointed out by the Vedic scholar Michael Witzel, it was also likened to Aditi (mother of gods, but literally boundless heaven), the earth (*prithvi*), the cosmic waters whose release by Indra established the cosmic law (*rta*), maternity, and poetry (*vac*), which was the monopoly of Brahmins. The cow, we are told, is used frequently in similes and metaphors and, it has been argued, these came to be taken literally in the course of time. But the cow was neither unslayable nor sacred in the Vedic period.

So, the Sangh Parivar's agenda today is one of selective or convenient revivalism? One of its ideologues, K.R. Malkani, espoused beef-eating publicly.

The views of the Sangh Parivar on the cow issue are unprincipled and hypocritical. K.R. Malkani, its one-time ideologue, said as early as 1966, without equivocation, that flesh of cows dying a natural death can be eaten. How does it go with the Parivar's foolish demand for a blanket national ban on cow slaughter?

The cow has become a great political symbol for the Hindu Right. How do you assess it historically? When did the cow become 'holy', and does this coincide with the onset of communalism in Indian history? Some historians have shown that the cow was a communalised animal even in the late 19th century.

Available evidence suggests that from the post-Mauryan period onwards the Brahminical attitude to cow-killing had begun to change. This may be explained in terms of both economic and religious developments. But one thing is clear, Brahminical texts now repeatedly began to state that the practice of cow-killing was not permissible in the Kali age. This accorded the cow a special place and made it unslayable.

So the unslayabilty of this animal would appear to be essentially a part of the Brahminical ideology, which in the early medieval period relegated beef-eating to untouchable castes, and the *Vyasasmriti* (I.12) clearly states a cow-killer to be an untouchable. But during the medieval period, the practice of killing cows came to be associated with Muslims and they were stereotyped as beef-eaters. Also there were occasional cow-related tensions. I am inclined to think that the cow, which may have been emerging as an emotive symbol among the Brahminical circles during the medieval period, became much more emotive with the rise of the Maratha kingdom and Shivaji, who was thought of as the protector of cows and Brahmins. But it was in the late 19th century that this animal was first used by the Sikh Kuka movement for mass political mobilisation against the British. At around the same time, in 1882 to be precise, Dayananda Saraswati founded the Gorakshini Sabha and he used it for uniting a wide variety of people against the Muslims. What was initially a Brahmin ideology now became a mark of Hindu identity.

The Sangh Parivar often dismisses professional history-writing in India and its conclusions. It says that Indian historians are way too influenced by Western historians and thus have failed to examine Indian culture and traditions properly. Indian historians have been called as 'sons of Macaulay and Marx' by proponents of Hindutva. Your comments.

The dismissal of history written by professional historians by the Sangh Parivar speaks volumes about its abysmal ignorance of both Indian and Western historiography. If you look at the trends of history-writing in India, especially after Independence, it will be abundantly clear that Indian historians have effectively questioned the basic tenets of colonial historiography and provided an alternative perspective for understanding India's past. On the other hand, look at the Sangh Parivar, which is clinging to the scheme of periodisation of Indian history into Hindu and Muslim periods, first enunciated by James Mill. Shouldn't we call its members children of James Mill then?

The Sangh Parivar has renewed efforts to falsely glorify early Indian practices and debunk the medieval period as it views both the periods only as 'Hindu' and 'Muslim' regimes respectively. What, according to you, are the problems with these divisions?

The division of Indian history into Hindu and Muslim periods is based on the assumption that the rulers belonging to the former time segment were all Hindus and those belonging to the latter were Muslims. But this is not true. There was no Hinduism or Hindu in ancient India. Ashoka, the most well-known ruler of ancient India, was a Buddhist and not 'Hindu'. Similarly, all rulers in the so-called Muslim period were not Muslims—the Cholas and Vijayanagara rulers were not Muslims!

This periodisation has also communalised the writing of Indian history and has led to undue glorification of the 'Hindu' period and to the unjustified denigration of the 'Muslim' period. A much better periodisation scheme can be evolved on the basis of the turning points in social, economic (including technological) and cultural history rather than on the basis of the fortuitous changes of the ruling dynasties. This can clarify many issues of social change over a long period.

The NDA government at the Centre has hardly shown any interest in exploring the British period or the colonial era despite its nationalist agenda. Why?

The NDA government's nationalism is a sham. It never engaged in anti-colonial struggle. And when it did, its most respected leader, 'Veer' Savarkar, was, in fact, so *veer* (brave) that he appealed to the British for clemency. Now the legacy of even those who fought for Independence is being either obliterated or diluted. Please recall Subramanian Swamy's tirade against the 'Nehruvian' historians.

There is a general consensus among professional historians across the world that any research on historical events, personalities, economies, society, etc., is best read bearing in mind the nature of the state in its times. A contextual research of historical events is deemed the most important way to study history. However, the Sangh Parivar's versions of history are veering towards what one can call 'de-contextualised history of individuals'. In this biographic approach towards history, Shahjahan, Aurangazeb and Mahmud of Ghazni become villains, and Hindu rulers like Maharana Pratap, Prithviraj Chauhan, etc., become heroes. Do you see a methodological problem in this kind of history?

This is related to my response to your previous question. Assessment of rulers should be done against the background of social, economic, cultural and other developments of their time. Decontextualised history will lead to the glorification of individuals like Prithviraj Chauhan and Maharana Pratap and the demonisation of Muslim rulers who defeated them in battle.

The proponents of Hindutva defend their versions of history by saying that professional historians are ideologically anti-Hindu and have never bothered to explore the syncretic traditions of Hinduism, while taking a keen interest in the traditions of other religions. Is this true?

This is far from true. Professional historians in India and abroad have devoted much attention to religious syncretism in ancient and medieval India. D.D. Kosambi, R.S. Sharma, Romila Thapar, Gunther-Dietz Sontheimer and a number of other scholars have analysed the syncretic tradition of India. But the votaries of Hindutva do not read, they only shout. They are a bunch of ignoramuses.

Index